Dear readers,

Almost one hundred and fifty years ago, an editor sat at a desk in an office in Dundee, a very short distance from where I am sitting as I write this. He was preparing to launch a new magazine, and feelings of both excitement and nervousness must have been flitting through his mind as he took a blank sheet of paper and began to address his readers for the first time.

If he could have seen the changes there have been in the way magazines are produced over the 150 years that separate us, I am sure he would be astounded. But I also hope very much that he would be reassured by all that hasn't changed – a reader's enjoyment of a good story, and the values of decency and kindness that have pervaded every page of "The People's Friend" in its 150-year history.

Since 1869, the "Friend" has witnessed global events and world wars, social upheaval and amazing inventions. It has seen monarchs come and go, men set foot on the moon and women gain the vote – but it has never lost its instinct for what its readers want from their magazine. It has reflected all of those changes, but it has always stayed true to its founding principles.

I am incredibly proud to be the editor of the world's longest running magazine as it celebrates its 150th anniversary. In our special commemorative edition, take a journey through time with the magazine that is truly a friend to all.

Angela

Angela Gilchrist, Editor.

Published in Great Britain by DC Thomson & Co. Ltd., Dundee, Glasgow and London. Editorial communications to "The People's Friend", DC Thomson & Co. Ltd., 2 Albert Square, Dundee DD1 1DD. © DC Thomson & Co. Ltd., 2018. While every reasonable care will be taken, neither DC Thomson & Co. Ltd., nor its agents will accept liability for loss or damage to any materials submitted to this publication.

Contents

In The Beginning

In January 1869, with
Queen Victoria on the throne, and
Prime Minister William Gladstone
in No. 10, Downing Street, a
publishing revolution was underway
in the Scottish city of Dundee.

7

ONE OF THE "PEOPLE'S FRIEND" PRINTING MACHINES.

This is not an ordinary orange

It is the small valuable "bitter" orange used in Keiller's Dundee Marmalade. Its rough skin is full of little cells, holding the aromatic juices which make Keiller's Marmalade so rich in flavour. The heart of the orange gives that slight but pleasant bitterness to Keiller's which makes this marmalade so appetising and so delicious.

KEILLER'S
DUNDEE
MARMALADE
FAMOUS FOR QUALITY FOR OVER 100 YEARS

Alamy.

City Of The Three Js

Dundee's famous nickname reflects the importance of three very different industries to its prosperity.

In the late 1700s, so the story goes, merchant's wife Janet Keiller invented marmalade while trying to use up a large quantity of bitter Seville oranges that had been acquired by her husband, John. What made Janet's recipe original was the inclusion of pieces of shredded orange peel.

Keiller's marmalade was a big hit with locals, and a factory was built in 1797 to meet demand. By the end of the 1800s jars of Keiller's were being shipped throughout the British Empire.

Jute And Journalism

A city dominated by women, an innovative newspaperman and an appetite for education and improvement proved a recipe for success.

FOR Dundee, the second half of the 19th century was a time of unprecedented growth. The population was increasing rapidly as industry boomed.

The city's location on the banks of the silvery River Tay made it accessible to lucrative overseas markets, and trade – in particular the jute trade – flourished.

Britain's jute industry was centred almost entirely on Dundee, and it was big business. At its peak, it employed 40,000 men, women and children in 125 mills.

Even the factories were huge; the Camperdown Works at Lochee, the largest textiles factory in Europe, was so vast it had its own railway station.

Of course, those mills and factories needed people to work in them, and folk flocked to Dundee in their droves seeking employment. In just 30

1869-1871

Nov 1869
The Suez Canal in Egypt opened, linking the Mediterranean Sea with the Red Sea.

iStock.

Nov 1869
The world's only remaining tea clipper, the *Cutty Sark,* was launched on Scotland's River Clyde.

iStock.

July 1870
On July 19 the Franco-Prussian War began, which was waged between the French Empire and a coalition of German States led by Prussia. The war was to last till the following year, resulting in the defeat of Napoleon III and his French forces, and shifting the balance of power in Europe.

Aug 1870
On August 4 popular Scottish entertainer Harry Lauder was born in Portobello, Edinburgh.

Alamy.

The River Tay brought trade and prosperity to Victorian Dundee.

years, from 1851 to 1881, the population of the city almost doubled to 140,000.

Unusually, it was Dundee's womenfolk on whom the city's prosperity was built. Of those 40,000 jute workers, 30,000 were women.

Since the jute industry had no bar on employing married women, more married women worked in Dundee than in any other British city.

This made domestic life very different from the norm; frequently, it was the men who stayed at home during the day and the women who were the breadwinners.

For single women in particular this was empowering. They had their own money, and were not dependent on men.

Publisher John Leng, who had been born in Hull, arrived into the midst of this unusual set of circumstances in 1851. He had launched his career

with the weekly "Hull Advertiser" at the age of nineteen, and just four years later he took up the role of editor of "The Dundee Advertiser", becoming managing partner a year later.

John Leng was a forward-thinking, bold and ambitious man who soon began to invest in the latest equipment and launch new publications.

In 1858 he started "The Dundee Perth And Forfar People's Journal", which soon became "The People's Journal".

He was also a hard-working and innovative publisher.

He was the first provincial editor to introduce illustrations in his newspapers, and he also made a point of recruiting women to edit, sub edit and write for his publications.

Then, in 1868, came the decision that was to create a publishing phenomenon. With "Journal" Editor

William Latto finding himself in the fortunate position of receiving more quality submissions than he could possibly publish, John Leng decided to launch a new monthly title as a companion.

"I want 'The People's Friend' to be recognised as the people's friend in hundreds of thousands of Scottish homes. I want it to be especially a friend of the mothers, wives, daughters and bairns of Scotland," he declared.

"I want it to be largely written by women for women, and by good women to make other women good. I want 'The People's Friend' from beginning to end to be full of matter that will both instruct and entertain.

"We welcome short stories, reminiscences and essays which bring out the Scottish character."

The first issue was edited by William Latto of "The People's Journal". Under his stewardship, "The

People's Friend" launched as "A Monthly Miscellany in connection with the 'People's Journal'" on Wednesday, January 13, 1869, priced one penny.

The first issue was produced from an office in Bank Street, Dundee, and comprised just 16 pages of tiny, close-packed black type, with not an image or illustration in sight.

Without preamble, the reader was plunged right into Chapter 1 of "Faithful And True – A Sad Story For The Happy Christmas Time" by Glaucus.

On page 8 of that first issue, the Editor made a pledge to his readers:

"We intend that fully one-half of the 'Friend' shall be devoted to fiction. . . The 'Friend' being intended for fireside reading, nothing will be admitted into its columns having the slightest tendency to corrupt the morals either of old or young."

"The People's Friend" had arrived! ■

Aug 1870
The British National Society for Aid to the Sick and Wounded in War was formed. Subsequently, the society changed its name to the British Red Cross, providing aid to victims of international conflicts and disasters, its red cross emblem recognised and respected the world over.

March 1871
On March 29 the Royal Albert Hall in London was opened by Queen Victoria.

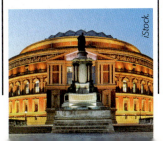

Aug 1871
Inventor and aeronautics expert Orville Wright was born in Dayton, Ohio. Along with his elder brother, Wilbur, the "fathers of modern aviation" became history-makers, conducting the first successful manned flight of a power-driven aeroplane, Flyer I, at Kitty Hawk, North Carolina, in 1903.

Dec 1871
On December 24, Italian composer Giuseppe Verdi's famed opera "Aida" was premiered in Cairo.

A Monthly Miscellany

Very quickly, Scotland's new magazine began to make a name for itself.

FOR the first year of its life, the "Friend" was published monthly, and contained a wide range of stories on a variety of topics.

A list of similes, written neatly in rhyming couplets to aid memory – "As heavy as lead – as light as a feather; As steady as time – uncertain as the weather" – appeared alongside a story entitled "The Celestial Visitor: A Mystery Of Paris", an article on "Early Marriages In Hindostan" and lots more. A great deal of reading was packed into just 16 pages.

Scottish content – often written in Scots – was very much to the fore, with poems such as "My Highland Home" by J.B.P., Glasgow, and "The Guid Broon Coat" written by G.W. Donald, Abbey Keeper, Arbroath, embodying the Editor's claim that the "Friend" would be "open to the contributions of the intelligent working men and women of Scotland."

Very quickly, as the magazine gained in popularity and became a success, regular features started to appear.

The first fiction serial, "Behind Life's Scenes: A Romance", began in the issue dated May 5, 1869, as did the "Books of the Month" column, which reviewed "Mrs Beecher Stowe's new novel 'Oldtown Folks'" and declared it "a sort of autobiography."

But it wasn't until January 5, 1870, that a single illustration was printed, and even then, the artwork was black and white and was incorporated into the cover masthead. Clearly those early readers had vivid imaginations!

The early issues contained much advice for women to help them be model wives and mothers.

Alongside musings on topics like "The Female Flirt", there were practical tips such as "Apples intended for dumplings should on no account have the pips taken out of them, as the pips impart a delicious flavour to the dumpling" and "Woollen clothes should be washed in very hot suds and not rinsed. Lukewarm water shrinks them."

However, there was recognition that a woman's life must be about more than endless domestic drudgery. Perhaps influenced by the numbers of working women in Dundee in the 1860s, the Essayist came up with a novel take on equality of the sexes with a discourse on "Occupations Of Utility For Women":

"Is it not a disgrace to this nation, which considers itself as standing at the head of all other nations, both in religion and morality, to allow men to intrude into occupations which de jure belong

Good Advice To Women (1869)

By a well-regulated household, by a well-informed mind, by gentleness and cheerfulness and love, render home delightful; the sweetest, happiest place to husband, and elder sons or elder brothers; so that it may be to them the most attractive place when seeking refreshment after toil, and rest from care. Surely this is no mean object to live for; a ministry which no woman should despise. It is her special mission.

1872-1875

Mar 1872
The Yellowstone National Park in Wyoming was established by US Congress, and the Yellowstone National Park Protection Act came into law.

Nov 1872
The brigantine *Mary Celeste* sailed from New York en route to Genoa, Italy. Less than a month later, the ship was spotted adrift east of the Azores, with no sign of her crew. Later, a boarding party discovered the crew's personal belongings and the ship's cargo still intact. Though the *Mary Celeste*'s lifeboat was missing, the crew were never found.

Jan 1873
French author Jules Verne's novel, "Around The World In 80 Days", was published.

April 1873
On April 4, the UK's Kennel Club was formed to ensure the welfare of dogs participating in shows and field trials.

exclusively to females, and thus snatching from them the means of obtaining their daily bread?"

An early sign that the fledgling magazine was spreading its wings came in issue dated March 3, with a word from the Editor:

"In consequence of the great success of the 'People's Friend' and the numerous letters of encouragement which have been addressed to us, we have resolved to obtain a special fount of new type, to be used exclusively in its columns.

"We have taken some pains to select the clearest, most elegant, and most readable type cast by Messrs Miller & Richard. It is now being made, and although we are not certain that the next number of the 'Friend' will be printed with it, we may promise that the number for May certainly will.

"We may again state that nothing will be wanting on our part to enhance the value and attractiveness of the 'Friend' to its already numerous array of readers."

It seems a considerable degree of investment was being made in the new title as confidence grew at John Leng. Miller & Richard was a world-famous type foundry in Edinburgh that supplied type to print firms around the globe.

Nothing but the best for the "Friend"!

As the magazine neared its first birthday, a decision was made.

"And so we launch 'The People's Friend' on its weekly voyages," the Editor wrote. "May it always be freighted with a valuable and acceptable cargo; and

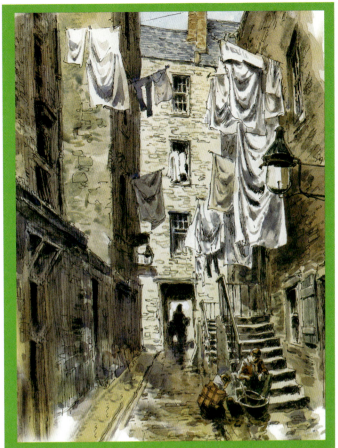

The Housewife

A character who was quickly to become a much-loved favourite in the early years of the "Friend" was introduced by the Editor in the first issue, with the announcement that "We shall have the Housewife discoursing from time to time on matters relating to domestic economy".

Sandwiched between items on rendering nitro-glycerine harmless and "how to cure a smoky chimney", this redoubtable person started as she meant to go on.

"It will be my duty to teach and yours to learn," she proclaimed in her debut column. However, "I shall be quite as willing to take hints as to give them. In this way both teacher and taught may be benefited . . . I do not despair of being able to make the Housewife a 'People's Friend' – one who is looked up to and loved 'for her work's sake'."

The Housewife certainly covered a diverse range of topics in those early years, offering advice on everything from the "Importance of Training Girls to Household Work" to "The Mischief of Wearing High-heeled Boots".

may prosperous winds never fail to send it safely to its haven in the hearts and homes of the People, whose Friend it seeks to become, and whose welfare it will always strive to promote." ■

The Birth Of The "People's Friend"

*We hail thy birth, thou promised one,
And trust this day thou hast begun
An honoured life, whase course will run
Through time unken'd,
Till thou hast proved, by victories won,
THE PEOPLE'S FRIEND.*

*While others strive for selfish fame,
Maintain the honour of thy name,
Fulfil the end for which thou came;
With might defend
The people's right, whene'er they claim
A PEOPLE'S FRIEND.*

*Resist the wrong, assist the right,
Neglected genius bring to light,
Save honest worth from party spite;
And aye contend
Against oppression's iron might –
THE PEOPLE'S FRIEND.*

*While thus an honoured life you lead,
And prove THE PEOPLE'S FRIEND indeed;
With wholesome food our minds aye feed,
Thrice noble end!
And show in this how much we need
A PEOPLE'S FRIEND.*

May 1873
David Livingstone, Scottish missionary and explorer of the African continent, died aged 60.

March 1874
The great escapologist and illusionist Harry Houdini (Ehrich Weiss) was born in Budapest, Hungary.

April 1875
On April 1, "The Times" published the first newspaper weather map, created by meteorologist Francis Galton. The synoptic chart, rather than showing the present forecast, highlighted conditions of the previous day, allowing readers to "predict" the day's weather based on this information.

Aug 1875
The author of "The Thirty-nine Steps", John Buchan, was born in Perth, Scotland.

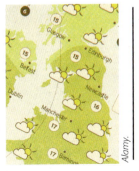

The firm bond between the magazine and its readers was key to its early success.

Our Design And Purpose

During the 1870s the "Friend" set about establishing its place in the hearts of its devoted and loyal readers.

THE "Friend" was now a weekly title, and readers wholeheartedly approved of the change. In the issue for April 6, 1870, the Editor wrote "A Special Notice To Our Readers": "We are proud to acknowledge the large and increasing popularity which 'The

People's Friend' has already achieved, and the many warm expressions of approval we are receiving almost daily."

This communication from the Editor was remarkable not least because, for many years, it was his custom to address his readers only once a year, in the New Year issue.

It's a measure of just how effusive the reaction from readers must have been.

The publishers had obviously hit on a winning formula and were sticking to it, with the same blend of fiction and features in every issue.

With the format set, they turned their attentions to cultivating a loyal and

growing legion of readers.

The aim was to make the "Friend" an indispensable part of its readers' lives. The magazine would be both friend and teacher, offering entertainment in the shape of stories such as "Mabel Mayfern: Or, The Gamekeeper's Revenge" alongside practical lifestyle and domestic advice on

1876-1880

March 1876

In March, Scottish-born inventor and scientist Alexander Graham Bell invented the telephone.

Alamy.

June 1876

On June 25, the American Battle of Little Bighorn, known as "Custer's Last Stand", was fought. Lieutenant Colonel George Armstrong Custer and his 7th US Cavalry were defeated by Native American tribes led by Sioux Chiefs Sitting Bull and Crazy Horse.

March 1877

The only time the annual boat race between Cambridge and Oxford Universities finished in a dead heat.

iStock.

Nov 1877

Anna Sewell's best-selling classic, "Black Beauty", was published in November, just five months before the author's death.

subjects as diverse as "How To Clean White Kid Gloves" and "Hints On Poultry Keeping", and informative essays on new and unusual topics such as "Sheep Farming In Buenos Ayres".

A "To Correspondents" page was introduced, with readers invited to send in their queries and requests.

The replies were then printed in subsequent issues, and this feature quickly became a firm favourite.

It was little wonder, then, that readers soon began to place their trust in the

Readers soon began to place their trust in the "Friend" to guide them through the pitfalls and challenges of modern life

"Friend" to guide them through the pitfalls and challenges of modern life, laying the foundations for the strong and loyal relationship between the magazine and its readers that has been such a mainstay of its success.

In fact, readers loved the magazine so much that they frequently wrote poems singing its praises!

As the decade wore on, new developments were

introduced. Each year, the Editor used his letter in the New Year Number to preview the improvements readers could expect to see in the next 12 months.

In 1874, he promised "The paper will be thicker, and it will be printed to 'register', on new type, and correctly folded."

In 1875, sheet music started to be printed in the magazine – the very latest in home entertainment for the times!

And also in this year, the Editor was keen to note that the magazine, like its readers, was striving for continuous improvement: "The fame of the 'Friend' has penetrated into all circles, and has been so favourably spoken of that writers of eminence and ability have been induced to offer contributions to its pages."

Proof came with a scoop – a story, "The Devil's Spectacles", specially written for the magazine by celebrated author Wilkie Collins.

The Editor's letter for the very last issue of 1879 set out a new approach for a new decade: "As it is our intention to reduce somewhat the space which has of late been given to serial stories, we shall have more room for short tales and literary papers, such as essays, sketches and descriptive pieces."

Careful evolution; listening to reader feedback, making small adjustments and improvements – right from its very earliest years, the "Friend" was in tune with what its readers wanted, and not afraid to move with the times to stay relevant to them. ■

A WEEKLY MISCELLANY
OF POPULAR AND INSTRUCTIVE LITERATURE.

Literary Leanings

In April 1870, a new tagline was added to the magazine's masthead: "A Weekly Miscellany of Popular and Instructive Literature". It soon became clear the "Friend" was on a mission to educate and inspire its readers with profiles of some of the greatest writers of English literature.

With articles on topics such as "John Clare, The Peasant Poet Of England", "The Man Shakespeare" and "Robert Burns And Masonry", readers were treated to extensive and knowledgeable discourses on the literary greats. Classic literature was not considered highbrow or elitist; it was for the everyday man and woman in the street.

There were personal recollections, too, from people who had met illustrious writers in person, with an "Anecdote Of Sir Walter Scott's Grandfather", musings on Walter Scott and Burns, and a memoir from Mr N.P. Dodge, who related his experiences of being a guest of Charles Dickens in "Home Life Of Charles Dickens": "At his own table Dickens was the best of talkers. No man ever told a better story."

Writers were the celebrities of their day, with every detail of their lives – such as "Tennyson And Tobacco" – of interest to curious readers.

Oct 1879

American Inventor Thomas Edison successfully trialled a commercially viable incandescent light bulb.

Dec 1879

On December 28, the central girders of Dundee's Tay Rail Bridge collapsed into the Firth of Tay, taking with them a train and the 70-plus passengers on board.

iStock.

June 1880

On June 27, Helen Adams Keller was born deaf-blind in Tuscumbia, Alabama. With the help of her sign-language teacher, Ann Sullivan, she learned to sign and communicate with the world around her. Helen went on to become a well-known literary figure, lecturer and leading advocate for those with disabilities.

Dec 1880

In southern Africa, the first Boer War broke out between British and Dutch settlers.

On The Cover

Victoria was on the throne, and round the globe Britain reigned supreme. Meanwhile, in Dundee, a new magazine was launched . . .

THE PEOPLE'S FRIEND

A Monthly Miscellany in connection with the "People's Journal."

No. 1. {REGISTERED FOR TRANSMISSION ABROAD.} WEDNESDAY, JANUARY 13, 1869. PRICE ONE PENNY.

THE STORY TELLER.

FAITHFUL AND TRUE—A SAD STORY FOR THE HAPPY CHRISTMAS TIME.

BY GLAUCUS.

"A sad tale's best for winter"—*Shakspeare.*

CHAPTER I.

There was a large party at dinner the day I arrived at Dolremmet Castle. Next day was the 12th of August, and the Earl of A—— had all his old friends about him, who for years had shot the grouse on his moors. The dinner party was like any other dinner party at a country house—perhaps a little merrier and less formal than most ones, as almost every one of the guests had already known each other well. The Countess was not yet an old woman, and did her duty of hostess very gracefully, as she formed the centre of a lively circle at the top of the table, while the Earl, a fine, hearty, middle-aged man, performed the duties of host as no one save an English gentleman knows how. Lady Fanny, the eldest daughter, whom I had the pleasure of taking into dinner, was a very old and firm friend of mine. Without being strikin[illegible] handsome, she was always considered good-looking. A clear, brilliant complexion, lots of dark hair, pearly teeth, a good figure, and a faculty for dressing well, were her chief characteristics, while a power of pleasant talk, combined with a keen appreciation of humour, rendered her a very agreeable companion. Opposite me sat Lady Edith, the most perfect representative of quiet English beauty. And yet, though her beauty was entirely English, in some respects it was difficult to describe. None of her features, except her eyes, were altogether perfect in themselves, but taken together they formed an exquisite harmony and delicacy of proportion. Looking across to her, and seeing her face dimpling into smiles, and her clear beautiful complexion changing its colour every moment, I think I never saw anything so fascinating. Her eyes were remarkably beautiful. The moment you looked into her face you were irresistibly drawn to her eyes, and they so fascinated you that you would gaze all the time she was talking to you into depths of quiet blue. They had all the silent beauty of those of a dumb animal, while at the same time they teemed with meaning, and were radiant with expression. On her right hand sat a young artist of great promise, who was employing his spare time at the Cas le in painting a likeness of Helen for the Countess, and who, to judge from his manner to her, was aided in his task not a little by a third party, who added not a little to the truth and beauty of the picture he painted. The only other person whom it is necessary for our story to recal at the table was the Hon. Augustus Weir, a nephew of the Earl's, and, as he had no sons of his own, the heir to his estates. It was generally understood that with her father's and mother's approval he was a suitor for Edith's hand, and on this particular occasion did not seem much to reli·h the attentions which the young artist lavished upon her, or the fond way in which she seemed to return them. After the ladies had retired, Rosetti—for so the artist was named—came over to my side of the table, wishing to strike up a friendship, as he had been a friend of my brother's in Rome, three years before. We soon got into a long and interesting talk about Rome, and the people we knew there; and my friend was describing with a true artist's ardour a new statue that had been discovered some short time before he left, when we were interrupted by Weir crying out from the other side of the table, loud enough for every one to hear—"When you fellows are done talking shop, I wish you would pass the wine." Rosetti immediately fired up, and had I not laid my hand on his arm and whispered a word in his ear, would have replied with some bitter sarcasm to the impudent remark. As it was, he passed the wine in silence, and Weir, though he had been drinking pretty freely, seeing he had gone a little too far, continued, "Well, the wine had been before you for at least ten minutes, and I thought you would never be done talking about that piece of cut stone," and, emptying his glass of port, continued, "For my part I can't see anything in these stone Venuses you rave about—healthy flesh and blood beauty for me." A reply was interrupted by the Earl crying out, "Well, Rosetti, have you yet found the proper shade of blue for fair Edith's eyes?" The shade of anger died away from the artist's face, and, smilingly, he replied, "Oh, sir, that would be impossible, but we have managed a little better to-day. Lady Edith was kind enough to put her whole afternoon at my disposal. She is so patient with me."

"A precious sight too much, Ed.," I heard Weir mutter between his teeth.

"Then," said the Earl, "we will join the ladies, and after tea we will go and have a peep at the picture."

We did so, and in about an hour afterwards found ourselves in the studio. As Rosetti drew aside the curtain before the picture, an exclamation of delight and surprise broke from the lips of every one present. As he arranged the lights so as to bring it out to advantage, the first impression of all of us was the life-likeness. After some little examination of it, what struck me most about the painting was not so much the evident genius which it displayed—although that was undoubtedly great—but the fond care with which the artist appeared to have lingered on every line and curve of expression, as if the brush had been reluctant to leave any one part of the picture, but fain would have lingered for ever on each. Every one was enchanted. Some congratulated Lady Edith, others the artist, and others the Earl, who stood silently gazing at the picture, but at last turning round to his daughter, he kissed her long and fondly, saying, "I never knew till now that my own darling Nelly was so lovely," and then, looking to the artist, "My dear Rosetti, we all owe you a debt of gratitude." Weir was the only one who had no complimentary word to say either to the painter or his subject. He had not yet quite recovered from the wine after dinner, and the mixture of jealousy and heated blood in his face was a sight not pleasant to see. On returning to the drawing-room, I had a long confidential talk with Lady Fanny about the evident *affaire de cœur* between her sister and the artist, and neither of us were able to forbode anything save sorrow and pain from the circumstance.

In pleasant enjoyment—shooting, fishing, riding, driving, playing croquet and Aunt Sally on the lawn, or, if the day was wet, knocking about the billiard balls—the days passed rapidly away. As the day for Rosetti's departure drew near, it was painful to see the two—Lady Helen and he—they were constantly together; and if in the crowded room they could not talk as they wished, the longing, wistful looks they exchanged were sad, and apparent to every one but the Earl and Countess, who evidently never dreamt of such a thing, or anything but friendliness between the two. Then the picture was constantly requiring some finishing touches, and in my room I could hear them conversing together in low tones, and sometimes I thought I heard a sob from the Lady Edith, as if some great sorrow was welling up in her heart. Saturday morning, the day on which he had to be up in town, came. We were assembled in the breakfast room, waiting for the Earl to come down and read prayers, when a message came desiring Sir John W—— to do so, as the Earl was engaged. Lady Edith, who was sitting next me, gave a great start. For a moment a deadly pallor came over her sweet face, and in the next it was suffused with a painful crimson. This was, however, unnoticed, and prayers were proceeded with. The Earl was in his usual place at breakfast, and made excuses for Rosetti, who, he said, was too busy making preparations for his departure to join us just yet. After the morning meal was over, I repaired to my bed-room to arrange some fishing tackle, and as I did so I heard a hurried passing to and fro in the studio. In a little I heard a rustle of silk and a timid knock at the door. It was immediately opened, and through my half-open door I could see Lady Edith enter. My tackle was either dreadfully entangled that day, or my mind was wandering on some other topic, for I took a long time to arrange it. Just as I was going out, I heard a great sob, and Rosetti exclaim—"Well, darling, I shall be faithful and true till death, and do you remember the Post Office of C——, In a second or two the door opened, and Rosetti hurried out, looking pale and haggard. As I knew Lady Edith could not be long in following, I half closed my door and waited. In a little she did come, walking listlessly, with her little head bowed on her bosom, which was heaving with "wild unrest," and her dove eyes were red with tears. I waited till she was fairly out of sight, and then, as I was going out, I thought I heard an exclamation of smothered rage from the studio. I looked in, but seeing no one, supposed it was mere delusion on my part. While I was waiting in the stable-yard for the rest of the fishing party, Weir came down and called out for his groom. His face had a strange mixture of rage, jealousy, hate, and triumph in it. I asked him if he was not going to join our party as he had intended, and he replied, 'No," that he had to go to a neighbouring town on some business. After we returned from our fishing excursion Fanny told me what I had already conjectured had happened. Rosetti had told the Earl of his love for Edith. The Earl told him in return that, however much he might have esteemed him as a friend and admired him as a genius, it would not be becoming to have him as a son-in-law, and that he had already promised his daughter Edith to Mr Weir.

Poor Lady Edith! from that day she was never her former bright and happy self. Sometimes at lunch she used to be a little like the old Edith, but in the afternoon, after her ride, which I noticed always took the direction of C——, she was always sad and despondent. The only pleasure she seemed to have was in caressing her fine St Bernard dog, Roma, which Rosetti had given her before leaving. The end of my stay at Dolremmet Castle had now come, and I could not help drawing a contrast between what it was when I first arrived and when I left, for Lady Edith's evident suffering was acutely felt by all in the house. In driving to the town, where I got my train, I had to pass through the village of C——. As I passed through, a thought suddenly struck me, and I bid the man drive to the Post Office, and found the rural postmaster, a civil, simple countryman, and inquired at him, in a casual way, if there were any letters for Lady Edith. He replied, "No, sir; I wish there were. The poor lady comes here day after day, and it makes my heart sore to say 'No!' to her. She takes on so, and turns away quickly to hide her face." As he said this, a door opened, and a woman, with an ugly, wicked face, asked what I had to do with Lady Edith's letters?—if there were any for her she would give them to her herself. I didn't reply, but, thanking the man for his civility, went away with a strange feeling of dissatisfaction and distrust at the woman's looks.

Christmas, dear old merry Christmas, with its gaieties and happy family meetings—above all, with its hallowed memories—found me once more at my old quarters in the Castle. There were a good many visitors besides myself—Mr Weir amongst the number. I was greatly shocked and grieved to see how ill poor Lady Edith was looking. The colour had quite died out of her face, and her features seemed pinched and wan. I heard from her sister that another trouble was weighing upon her. Mr Weir had again begun his attentions to her, and the Earl had been pressing her to fix an early month for her marriage with him. She put her father off from week to week, pleading ill health; but she was beginning to see that this would not always do. In her sorrow she seemed like some poor little flower, which, rudely shaken with wind and rain

Jan 13, 1869

Sir John Leng's new monthly periodical was to be essentially Scottish, with fully one half devoted to fiction and based on good family values.

"The 'Friend' being intended for fireside reading, nothing will be admitted into its columns having the slightest tendency to corrupt the morals of old or young."

Jan 1, 1873

The aim was to inspire readers as well as entertain.

March 11, 1874

Alexander Anderson (Surfaceman) was a noted poet.

March 31, 1875

This exciting serial story smacked of Charlotte Brontë.

Jan 14, 1880

An early effort from a much-loved contributor.

The Victorians

It was an exciting era of education and improvement, of scientific discovery and social advancement. And the "Friend" had its part to play . . .

The Age Of Science

Victorian Britain saw an unprecedented explosion in scientific discovery, and the "Friend" was determined to keep its readers up to date.

Pedal Power

1 Victorians were conscious of the bicycle's benefits for body and mind, and were also keen to find ways to improve the design. Hence the above bicycle for travelling on ice.

2 If you weren't keen on cycling, then "perhaps the pneumatic skate may enable even old fogies to indulge in a little skim through the air."

FROM 1837 to 1901, Victoria's reign was a time of immense change in the world, with Britain's Empire at its peak and both incredible wealth and stark poverty at home. Science fiction writers like H.G. Wells began to imagine what the world of the future would look like, and Charles Darwin proposed his theory of evolution, whilst electricity started its steady march into our lives.

It was a time stuck between superstition and speculation and the modern age, when science blossomed but went in a dozen directions all at once, some of which would prove dead ends.

Take the science of phrenology, the idea that the shape of your head could determine aspects of your personality. The "Friend" took a look at the "bump of avarice", apparently a common

cause of thievery.

The railways were enjoying a golden age, although there was speculation whether or not there would ever be

For the Victorians, dynamite helped them travel the world – blasting out tunnels, canals and roads

meaningful heating in the carriages. Rail staff had taken to passing hot-water bottles to passengers during the winter months.

Balloons ruled the skies,

although it was really the weather that ruled the balloons. Who knew where you would end up?

"The helplessness of balloons, and the small progress that has been made within the century of their existence in rendering them available for locomotion, have often been alluded to but generally, for the purpose of asserting the impossibility of Man's being ever able to navigate the air at will."

It seemed unlikely that we'd truly conquer the skies.

Much more promising was the beginning of a Channel Tunnel in 1881. Though progress was made on both sides, the attempt was abandoned in 1882 due to worries about compromising national security, with the Napoleonic Wars in the not-too-distant past.

The "Friend" was in no doubt that electricity would

1881-1885

Aug 1881
On August 6, bacteriologist and founder of penicillin Alexander Fleming was born in Ayrshire, Scotland.

Oct 1881
The legendary shoot-out at the OK Corral took place in Tombstone, Arizona. It involved lawman Wyatt Earp and his brothers Virgil and Morgan, alongside Doc Holliday, against the Clanton/McLaury gang. The inspiration behind numerous Hollywood films, the shoot-out itself lasted a mere 30 seconds.

Jan 1882
On January 18 A.A. Milne, author and creator of Winnie-the-Pooh, was born in London.

June 1882
Mathematician Henry W. Seely's electric clothes iron was patented, marking the end of stove-heated irons.

Mankind's early attempts to conquer the skies were at the mercy of the weather.

change our world.

"We live in an age of wonders, for we see one after another the mighty forces of the universe, like vanquished princes, approaching to do service to their great and potent emperor, Man."

In such eloquent language the "Friend" welcomed the imminence of the electric light, turning night into day.

There was even a scheme afoot to put in place a chain of lightships across the Atlantic Ocean, with one every ten miles connected by electric cable to guide ships safely across the open ocean.

Another invention which defined the era was dynamite – the more explosive bigger brother to gunpowder.

For the Victorians, it helped them travel the world – blasting out railway tunnels, canals and roads – while gunpowder had already changed

warfare for ever.

"If wars have not become less common, they are, as a whole, less brutal and sanguinary."

With the Crimean and Boer wars taking place during this time, it was a

It was the era of Darwin's ground-breaking and often controversial theories on evolution

hot topic. Gunpowder almost seemed a welcome invention, at least until somebody built the first automatic machine gun in 1884.

It was the era of Darwin's ground-breaking theories – "there never can be any reason for fearing the progress and elucidation of

truth" – and in describing a little of his background the "Friend" explained why it was such a remarkable age of discovery.

In the mid-Victorian era "the battle clouds were being blown away from the

bloody fields of Europe, and civilisation was entering on a period of advance and reconstruction."

In this time, great minds of science were free to turn their powers to the pressing concerns of the day.

The early progress of Dr

Robert Koch in appearing to have found the means to overcome tuberculosis brought hope for millions. It was a disease that reached epidemic proportions by the 1850s and was still common in the later part of the century.

Unfortunately, although Dr Koch recognised the cause, it would be well into the next century before a true cure would be found.

At its peak, one in seven people would die from the disease.

Health care was making rapid progress, though, and in the "Friend's" pages you could find advice on giving drowned folk chest compressions to restore them and news of the emergence of a successful rabies vaccine in 1885.

Though woe betide you if you were blind around "Friend" readers, after the magazine told them that the surest cure was a sudden unexpected blow to the head! ■

May 1883

On May 24, the Brooklyn Bridge opened, linking the New York boroughs of Brooklyn and Manhattan.

Oct 1883

The Orient Express ran between Paris and Romania, its passengers destined for Constantinople (Istanbul). Associated with opulent and romantic rail travel through some of Europe's finest cities, over the years the train's famous passengers included Tsar Nicholas II, Marlene Dietrich and Agatha Christie's Hercule Poirot.

Dec 1884

Mark Twain's "Adventures Of Huckleberry Finn" was published, ensuring the writer's position in the annals of American literature.

Sept 1885

On September 12, Arbroath beat Bon Accord 36-0, resulting in the highest score in professional football in Britain.

A Changing Landscape

As industrialisation gathered pace, so, too, did the rise in the middle class – with etiquette and morals the watchwords of the day.

As Britain forged ahead with industrialisation, the new working ways brought the expansion of towns and cities, with fewer people than ever living in the country. Along with industrialisation came a rise in the middle classes, as many grabbed the opportunity to make the most of the rapidly changing times.

Money alone, however, was not enough. Etiquette, high moral values and a need to better oneself was never more apparent than in the Victorian era.

Self-improvement and reading were encouraged, nowhere more so than in the "Friend".

"Books and periodicals should be angels in every household. They are urns to bring us the golden fruit of thought and experience from other minds and other lands . . ."

Reading aloud to family members also promised "refinement and dignity".

Popular literary works included those by Charles Dickens, Lewis Carroll and Louisa May Alcott, author of "Little Women". The latter's death was recorded in the "Friend" with the words "American literature is distinctly the poorer".

The "Friend" also paid homage to "Three notable women of recent times" –

Mary Russell Mitford, Elizabeth Barrett Browning and Janet Hamilton.

"It is not so difficult now to find women who can do something more than sing, play, sketch and sew ornamental work . . . we find unmarried women with property claiming their

The domestic role was taken seriously and advice on the "right" way to run the home was in abundance

right to have a vote. The three women we speak of now are an ornament to their sex – true and noble women – while each one of

Dedicated Followers Of Fashion

Tight corsets at this time helped to cinch in ladies' waists in the cause of fashion, but this practice also restricted breathing, so fainting wasn't uncommon.

This inventive bustle and chair combination may have offered support in a moment of weakness, but the patent came to nothing when the idea didn't take off!

1886-1890

May 1886
In May, John S. Pemberton created Coca-Cola and sold the bottles in a pharmacy in Atlanta, Georgia.

Alamy.

Oct 1886
The Statue of Liberty was dedicated as a gift of friendship from France to America.

iStock

June 1887
The Golden Jubilee of Queen Victoria took place, celebrating her 50th anniversary on the throne.

iStock

Nov 1887
Arthur Conan Doyle's "A Study In Scarlet" was published in "Beeton's Christmas Annual". This marked the inaugural appearance of legendary detective Sherlock Holmes and his trusty associate Dr Watson.
The fictional duo created by Conan Doyle would subsequently appear in a further three novels and several short story collections.

them was distinguished in her own special department."

On the whole, however, a woman's place was very much in the home. Queen Victoria, described as "the mother of the nation", was seen by many as a good role model.

The domestic role was taken seriously and advice on the "right" way to run the home was in abundance – "Mrs Beeton's Book of Household Management" proved a hit with Victorian women. The "Friend", too, was more than happy to help guide its readers with the advice they sought.

Everything from food to fashion came under scrutiny. The perils of overcooked food was highlighted to the woman of the house.

"You might as soon expect to obtain nourishment from the fibres of dead wood as from the 'rags' of beef or mutton."

And health advice on a "Summer Diet" would stand up well even today: "Eat sparingly of meat . . . let the diet consist chiefly of grains, fruits and vegetables. Drink no stimulants – not even tea or coffee."

There was even advice on "How to avoid being an old maid", the maid described as being "clothed in garments generally too juvenile by some ten years, or else misfitting . . . the face emerging from these garment is sour and hard in its normal expression."

But sage advice was also offered to gentlemen.

"Man seldom prospers in the world without the

Tracking Progress

Railways not only allowed for the easy transportation of goods which helped the smooth running of trade and industry, but also allowed people to travel around more freely thanks to cheap rail travel.

One particular route between Glasgow and Greenock carried passengers a distance of 23 miles for ninepence third class, one shilling second, and one shilling and threepence first class.

Rail travel brought about a huge rise in day trips and holidays to the seaside, where people could enjoy the sea air, Punch and Judy shows and donkey rides. It was certainly a way of escaping the "pea-souper" fogs of pollution that were blighting the big cities. The "Friend" noted that "sootiness" in London was "causing not only great inconvenience, but serious mortality among the asthmatic and bronchially-affected inhabitants of the metropolis."

One way to escape the city pollution would have been to take up the growing pursuit of cycling. But it was the brave new woman who dared indulge in this pastime, with one enthusiast writing in the "Friend": "What though the frolicsome wind has been taking liberties with her hair . . . my dear girls, get rid of the idea that there is anything unladylike in the mere act of riding a bicycle. The girl who cycles may be every whit as sweet and womanly as the prim young schoolroom miss."

co-operation of his wife."

The "Friend" also advised that polite requests should be adopted towards children and servants, as opposed to giving orders, "merely because we have the authority to command".

But things were changing

The social divide between the classes was never more apparent

and middle-class girls began to move with the times. Rather than choosing careers as governesses or teachers, they began seeking employment as typists or went into nursing.

Florence Nightingale did much to inspire others to choose the latter profession. Many working-class girls went into service, answering the need of the flourishing middle classes.

The social divide between the classes was never more apparent. The working class had to eke out a living as best they could, the fear of the workhouse looming should they fall on even harder times. Poor sanitation and overcrowding took their toll and infant mortality was high.

However, the Victorian era was also known as the age of reform, with many pushing to improve the lot of the poor. ∎

Jan 1888

The National Geographic Society was formed, ensuring "the increase and diffusion of geographical knowledge".

March 1889

On March 31, two years after construction began, the building of Paris's iconic Eiffel Tower was completed.

July 1890

Irish raconteur Oscar Wilde's only novel, "The Picture Of Dorian Gray", was published. Born in Dublin in 1854, Wilde was also a poet, short story writer and dramatist, and his play "The Importance Of Being Earnest" established him as a leading playwright of the time. He died in 1900, aged 46.

Sept 1890

On September 15, best-selling crime author Agatha Christie was born in Torquay, Devon.

The "Friend" began showing its readers the joys of travel in Europe.

Exploring The World

As the British Empire expanded, the "Friend" was quick to encourage its readers to seek new horizons.

AFTER the Napoleonic Wars left France in a weakened position, Britain became a dominant global power, with an overseas empire that expanded to hold sway over a fifth of the world's population.

Throughout Victoria's reign people were encouraged to pour into Britain's overseas territories in order to populate them and solidify Britain's hold on them.

"It is well that the teeming population of the United Kingdom can grow and expand beyond the confines of our 'sea-girt isle'. It is a fortunate and providential arrangement which is becoming more and more necessary as the years roll onward," the "Friend" remarked.

Stories of life in the colonies were full of enthusiasm. A Tasmanian ex-pat wrote to the "Friend" about living in Hobart: "I live on the fattest of the land. Milk is beneath our notice; nothing but cream of the consistency of butter pleases us."

New Zealand had a bright future ahead of it, the "Friend" asserted confidently, as did Fiji, providing it had enough "skilled capitalists to turn to advantage the natural productivity of the land." Fiji was annexed to Britain formally in 1874.

The "Friend" staff and writers were most enamoured with Australia, which offered "as wide and hopeful a field for the intending emigrant at present as any other part

1891-1901

April 1891

Showman P.T. Barnum, owner of the "Greatest Show On Earth" travelling circus, died aged 80.

May 1894
Blackpool Tower opened to the public. It measured 518 feet from the ground to the top of the tower's flagpole, and the original admission charge was 6d. The tower's iconic ballroom once had strict rules such as "Gentlemen may not dance unless with a lady" and "Disorderly conduct means immediate expulsion".

Apr 1897
On April 19, the world's oldest city marathon was first run in Boston, Massachusetts.

May 1897
Bram Stoker's "Dracula" was published. Though Stoker wrote 12 novels in his lifetime, the Gothic horror was considered his masterpiece.
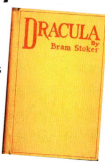

of the earth's surface" – especially after gold was struck.

South America was a tough nut for Brits to crack, but British Columbia was a land of plenty – and likely to blossom once the Canadian Pacific Railway was completed. It was finished in 1885, which had a significant impact on Granville, the line's western terminus, soon to be renamed Vancouver.

"Any smart, active capable man is sure to succeed in Canada," the magazine noted, going on

Throughout Victoria's reign, people were encouraged to pour into these overseas territories

to stress he also needed a strong constitution and to be "blessed with a common-sense wife used to country work."

Between 1801 and 1871 the population of Britain doubled, with migrants coming to the UK faster than Brits were moving abroad. A growing middle class meant a huge rise in demand for domestic servants, now one of the biggest sectors of employment.

As folk made their fortune in overseas

territories, demand for domestic staff grew from Canada to Australia, too, speeding up the spread of Brits overseas.

The growing middle class also had more leisure time, and the "Friend" began showing its readers the joys of travel in Europe, with trips to Norway, Switzerland, Athens and Palermo amongst the destinations.

In many places, the hotels had only just had their final lick of paint as the international tourism boom began at pace.

"The ideal holiday implies a thorough change – not only of air and scene, but also of occupation," the magazine advised, encouraging busy folk to take it easy, and office workers to try something strenuous.

Britain's seaside resorts had never been more popular, and the scenic lands of what would become known as the Lake District and other future national parks were accessible by train or boat and thronged with Victorian visitors.

The prospect of foreign travel was exciting, but it was easy to come a cropper if you were not comfortable with the local language and customs.

The magazine related with humour the story of the woman who tried to ask for milk in Spain and ended up with tickets for a bullfight, and the gentleman in France who thought he'd asked the maid not to let the fire go out, but had actually asked her not to let the madman out, and found himself locked in for the day. ■

Famous Names

The "Friend" has never been the place for celebrity news, but some Victorian names were simply too important for the magazine to pass by.

One hundred years after his death, the Robert Burns Centenary Supplement was found inside the "Friend" of 1896, celebrating his work and speculating what would have happened had he made it to a riper age than his thirty-seven years.

The true story of someone's Aunty Eppie who had inadvertently shared a drink with Mr Burke of Burke and Hare fame was too good not to print, while the "Friend" mourned the passing of social commentator and author Thomas Carlyle

with two full pages on his life's works.

The "Friend" wrote extensively of its high hopes for author J.M. Barrie, who only four years before an appearance in the magazine had been an "unknown". The magazine touted him as one to watch years before the character of Peter Pan made it into the public eye.

Not all the names would have meant something to "Friend" readers, though. Isaac Pitman, for example, was the inventor of a system of shorthand. "A benefactor to the English speaking race", the magazine declared in 1887. Perhaps to journalists, but maybe not a household name for readers!

JAMES MATTHEW BARRIE.

Dec 1898

Scientist Marie Curie discovered radium. Earlier that year, she had discovered polonium, named after her home country of Poland.

July 1899

On July 21, novelist Ernest Hemingway was born. Hemingway served in the Great War as an ambulance driver, and his experiences provided inspiration for his novel "A Farewell To Arms". Hemingway also wrote "For Whom The Bell Tolls" and the Pulitzer Prize-winning "The Old Man And The Sea".

Feb 1900

The Kodak Brownie camera was launched, bringing affordable snapshot photography to the public.

Jan 1901

The Commonwealth of Australia Constitution Act came into force, uniting the Australian states under a Federal Commonwealth.

On The Cover

The "Friend" reflected the Victorians' fascination with invention . . .

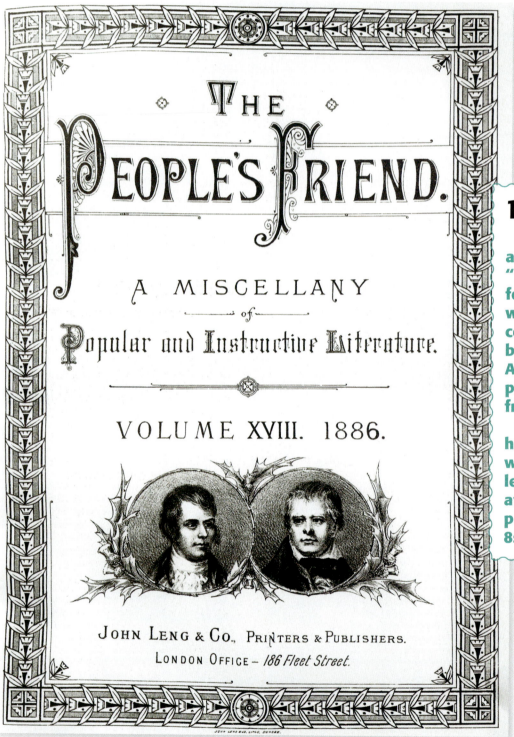

1886 Volume

Cloth cases to bind a year's worth of the "Friend" were sold for 1s 6d each. They were offered in four colours – red, blue, brown and green. An index and title page could be had free of charge.

Complete volumes, handsomely bound with gilded lettering, were also available for purchase at a cost of 8s 6d.

July 6, 1881

This issue seems to be part of a monthly volume.

Jan 12, 1891

The pictorial masthead showed a range of interests.

Jan 19, 1891

A poem to the beautiful Dora opened this issue.

March 14, 1898

For protection from winter's ills, drink Bovril!

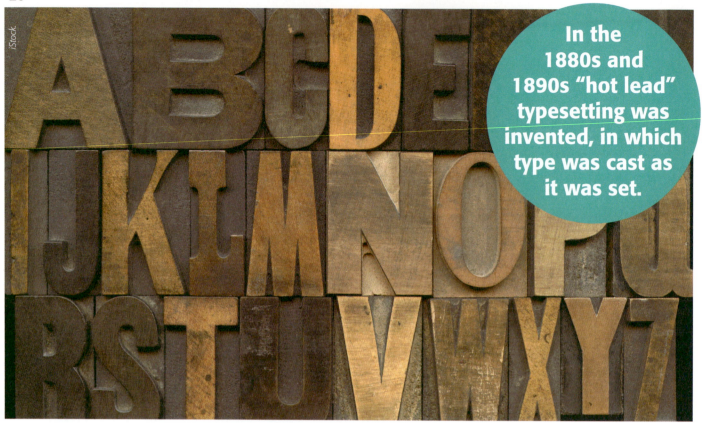

iStock

In the 1880s and 1890s "hot lead" typesetting was invented, in which type was cast as it was set.

Hot Metal

Printing methods have changed radically in the 150 years since the "Friend" first launched.

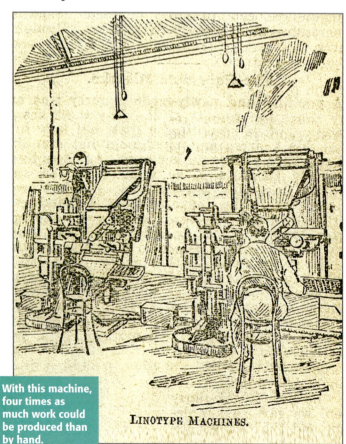

LINOTYPE MACHINES.

With this machine, four times as much work could be produced than by hand.

FROM the year of its birth, the "Friend" was singled out, with no expense spared to give the readers all they could desire in this remarkable new publication.

One early innovation came with the acquisition of a special font: "We have taken some pains to select the clearest, most elegant, and most readable type cast by Messrs Miller & Richard."

Although in modern usage "font" is almost synonymous with "typeface" – Times, Ariel, Helvetica, etc. – in metal typesetting a font, or fount, was a particular size, weight and style of typeface. A typeface consisted of a range of fonts that shared an overall design.

In traditional typesetting the font would be made from metal or wood, while today the font is a digital file. Some metal type, such as dashes, spaces and line-height spacers, was not part of a specific font, but rather generic pieces capable of being used with any font.

Line spacing is still often called "leading" because the strips used were made of lead, softer than the traditional forged-metal pieces and compressing more easily when locked together.

In the 1880s and 1890s "hot lead" typesetting was invented, in which type was cast as it was set, either piece by piece with Monotype or in whole lines of type at one time, as with Linotype ("line o' type").

Each line was cast as a continuous block, a boon for rapid newspaper printing. It was used as standard for mass-market printing from the late nineteenth century, declining with the phototypesetting, and then the changing electronic processes between the 1950s and 1980s.

In 1903 the "Friend" gave the exciting news that the magazine was to be permanently enlarged to 24 pages (28 including the cover). The typesetting was to be done by one of the latest Linotype machines – "A marvel of mechanical skill".

The Linotype machines were powered by electricity, and much was made of the speed with which they turned out columns of type. It was calculated that a Linotype worked by one man could set up the equivalent of 7000 letters per hour, equal to about four times the work that could be done by hand composition.

The magazine would be printed from fresh type each week, while paper of a heavier texture "specially

The magazine would be printed from fresh type each week, while paper of a heavier texture "specially made for the 'Friend'" was to be used

made for the 'Friend'" was to be used. This rendered the magazine easier to read, and the extra pages would "admit a wider and more varied supply of reading material".

The Editor proudly claimed there would be an increase in the number of illustrations, always a popular feature, and many new features would from time to time be introduced.

He also stressed the advantages of the "Friend" having a paper mill of its own – the new paper was to be made at Donside Paper mills near Aberdeen, belonging to Messrs John Leng and Company.

"Thus, as we hope and believe, by these desirable and well-considered alterations, the 'People's Friend' will be fully

The Monster

The 1903 reader was treated to a charming account of a morning in the printing room . . .
We are standing in the machine-room surrounded by half a dozen of the finest printing machines in the country. Upon some of these machines are printed the "People's Journal" and on others the People's Penny stories, Aunt Kate's Handbooks and other publications that are constantly going out from John Leng & Co.'s great publishing house, each machine costing as much money as might purchase a small estate.

In the early morning the stereotypers have been busy, and the stereotype plates, each accurately rounded to fit the cylinders of the machine, come down from the upper regions in a hoist.

A staff of printers and mechanics – one and all splendid representatives of their ancient craft – are waiting to deal with the plates, and they are applied to the machine.

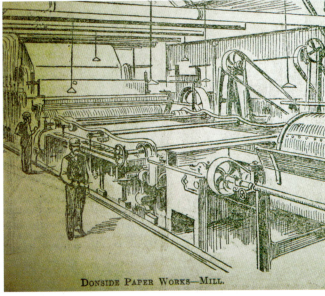

DONSIDE PAPER WORKS—MILL.

During these operations it is not unlikely that a member of the firm will come down to see how things are going on, for Messrs John Leng & Co. are in the closest personal touch with every department of their great establishment.

At length everything is ready; a bell rings, slowly the sleeping monster wakes up and growls horribly, the wheels revolve and, oh! what an infernal din they make!

The printing-presses, now thoroughly roused up, settle down to their day's task. At one end paper goes in, at the other end the "People's

Friends" are delivered, printed, folded, stitched, cut and counted in dozens at the rate of 20,000 copies an hour.

Wonderful, isn't it? What Arabian tale or classic story is like unto this? But just as there is no making of omelettes without breaking of eggs, so there is no doing of this tremendous amount of work without a tremendous amount of noise, so after a few minutes we are glad to ascend to quieter regions, with the growl of the subterranean monster growing ever fainter in our ears.

maintained in the foremost place which it has long held as a popular journal of healthy and enjoyable reading for every member of the household."

The Editor couldn't be accused of moving too quickly – the last important change had come in the form of a new cover, and that in 1894!

But a precedent had been set, and for the next 110 years the publishers of the "Friend" would continue to keep up with modern technology and new working methods, including the purchase in 2013 of a £25m printing press.

It was officially opened by the Duke and Duchess of Rothesay, and D.C. Thomson's Chairman

Andrew F. Thomson had this to say: "We are investing significant sums in publishing and we're proud to be investing in the future of print. By investing, modernising and developing our titles using

this capability, we increase efficiency, providing more for our customers. It also allows us to create new opportunities for the business and stands us in good stead for the future."

No change there! ∎

HRH Prince Charles, The Duke of Rothesay, tries out the new state-of-the-art printing press.

"PEOPLE'S FRIEND" LITERARY DEPARTMENT.

The Violin Man

One member of the "Friend" staff still delights with his wit and knowledge a hundred years after his passing.

WILLIAM C. HONEYMAN, author of "The Violin: How to Master It," &c.

WILLIAM CRAWFORD HONEYMAN was born in 1845, and he had a column in the magazine entitled "For Violin Players" which ran between 1897 and 1909.

He gave advice to budding players, as well as makers of violins, who sent in their efforts for his expert opinion.

A skilled musician himself, his remarks were always amusing (and often scathing), though he was quick to bestow praise and encouragement where deserved.

But Honeyman had several strings to his bow. Under the name James McGovan he published a number of books in the 1870s which purported to be the autobiographical writings of a policeman in Edinburgh.

Several more stories appeared in the "Friend" in the 1880s under the title "Experiences Of An Edinburgh Detective".

The character Honeyman created is possibly one of the first detectives in the crime-writing fiction genre.

Arthur Conan Doyle, at that time a student in Edinburgh, would almost certainly have come across his books.

Although the violin queries stopped by 1910, advice for this lovelorn "Friend" reader by a mysterious figure called "The Oracle" would seem to have been penned by a very familiar hand:

The "Friend" Office, 1905

FIFTEEN (whose spelling might be better) has an ambition, which is to write a violin column like this one, and he wants to know how it is done.

It is the easiest thing in the world. You merely come into this office and find four or five fiddles lying on a shelf, and tuck them under your arms, and carry them up a very narrow stair, with people rushing down in a hurry pretending to smile and like it when you jab them in the stomach with the ends of the fiddle cases; and then go into a room where a bundle of letters lies waiting your arrival.

You look at all the fiddles and try them carefully, with an editor at your back trying vainly to write his leader for the day and make it lively and amusing, while tearing his hair out over the distracting sounds of those fiddles.

As soon as the fiddles are tried and written about, however, the editor gets his innings, for you have to read and answer your letters while he has an old man visitor who wants to put him right in politics, so that your answers may get mixed with tariff and Home Rule questions, which is never noticed till you are told that another compositor has gone mad trying to make sense of your copy.

Oh, it is delightful! Come in, Fifteen, and have a shottie at it; but first of all you should brush up your spelling. They are all prejudiced in this office against bad spellers, so it might be just as well to humour them.

"VERA,
"Better let things drift. He may not have tired of you, but it looks as if he had.

"The Oracle would have tired of you long ago; he dislikes shuffling, particularly feminine shuffling.

"His motto has always been, 'better a finger aff than aye waggin',' but some men are more patient — sheepish, the Oracle calls it."

Honeyman died on April 14, 1919, at his home in Newport. The Dundee "Courier" paid tribute to him.
FAMOUS DETECTIVE-NOVELIST FOUND DEAD "JAMES MCGOVAN"
By the death of Mr William C. Honeyman, which took place yesterday at Cremona Villa, Newport, Tayside has lost a notable novelist and a great violin authority.

Well known as William C. Honeyman, he was yet more widely known as James McGovan, the name under which his series of detective stories was written. As one of the pioneers of the detective story James McGovan found favour with the reading public.

Though born in New Zealand, Mr Honeyman practically belonged to Edinburgh, and that city afforded setting for the majority of his stories.

Tender-hearted, yet a caustic critic, Mr Honeyman was as ready to give generously when his sympathy was evoked as he was to ridicule friends as well as foes on points that did not meet with his approval. ∎

WM LUCAS:
For a first attempt at violin making this is wonderfully good. Value of violin £2. Many thanks for 1s to the Love Darg.

NIL DESPERANDUM:
The cause of your slide sounding like a cat when it is trodden on is that you have been doing it slowly instead of swiftly. It can be done quite as well on a cheap factory fiddle as on the best Cremona that ever was made, so don't blame your fiddle, blame the man at the end of it.

JOHN LUTON:
Your violin is worth £3. The office boy failed to carry up your fiddle, and your present to him was therefore ruthlessly confiscated. This is sad at New Year, but one must be cruel only to be kind.

JAMES B. MURRAY:
Your violin is beautifully made and finished; the scroll is rather plain, the tone is large and firm and of a brilliant quality. Value £6. Shall be pleased indeed to see your latest production. You are a born violin-maker.

PETER B:
Writes that he sees a great many cases in this column of fiddlers in difficulty through being in love, but his difficulty is that he has never been in love, and wants to know how he can get over it? Go away, Peter, you don't know when you are well off.

LIZZIE:
Your idea of the writer of this column is pretty correct, except that he is rather bald, the cause being young ladies asking too many questions. He does not paste the hairs over the bald place, as your father does, and thinks no-one should.

FORDELL, WANGANNI:
Your letter is very gratifying. Honeyman's Gully, now a part of Wellington, was so named because the father of the writer of this column built the first house in that place.

In the early days, when fund-raising took the form of an exhibition, there would also be fund-raising concerts and dinners. Notable people would be asked to open the bazaar. Later on, the Love Darg entries would go on show. These events would see tables piled high with toys, babywear, children's garments and adult knitwear.

Sometimes there would be 50 or more items supplied by one industrious person. "Friend" staff would be on hand to help.

IN the November 4, 1885 issue the "Friend" made an announcement. "GRAND JUVENILE COMPETITION AND EXHIBITION. It is now our intention to hold a GRAND EXHIBITION AND BAZAAR OF JUVENILE INDUSTRY, the proceeds of which will be applied towards forming the nucleus of a fund for naming a Cot in the Children's Ward of the Dundee Royal Infirmary to be known as the PEOPLE'S FRIEND JUVENILE COT."

Girls were invited to send "Sewed Work, Knitting and Crochet, Fancy Work and Cookery", and boys were asked to contribute "Models, Joiner Work, Cabinet Work, Drawing and Penmanship".

This competition, purely

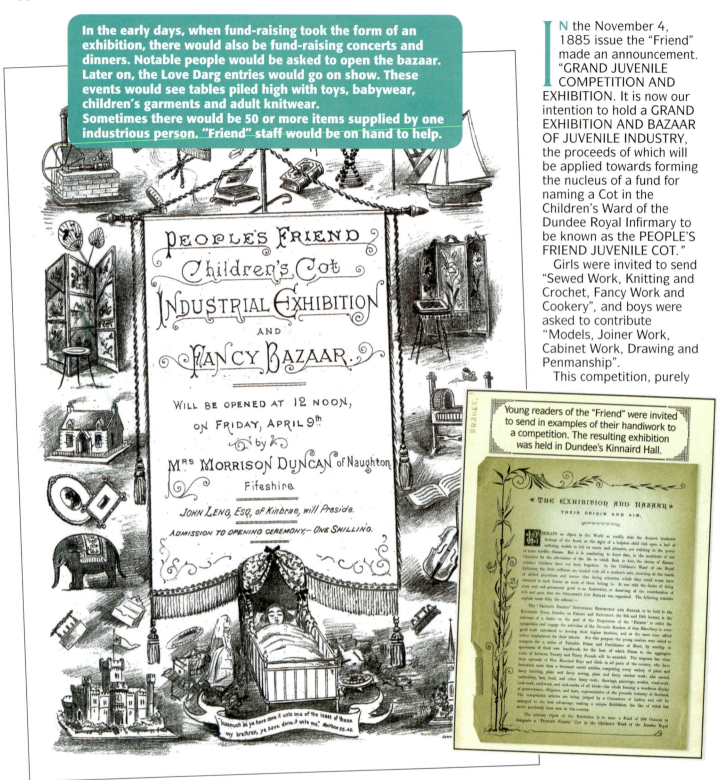

PEOPLE'S FRIEND
Children's Cot
INDUSTRIAL EXHIBITION
AND
FANCY BAZAAR.

WILL BE OPENED AT 12 NOON,
ON FRIDAY, APRIL 9th
by
Mrs MORRISON DUNCAN of Naughton,
Fifeshire.

JOHN LENG, ESQ, of Kinbrae, will Preside.

ADMISSION TO OPENING CEREMONY.— ONE SHILLING.

"Inasmuch as ye have done it unto one of the least of these my brethren, ye have done it unto me." Matthew 25.40.

Young readers of the "Friend" were invited to send in examples of their handiwork to a competition. The resulting exhibition was held in Dundee's Kinnaird Hall.

A Day's Work Done For Love

The Love Darg is the magazine's own charitable appeal.

for young readers of the "Friend", was the forerunner of today's Love Darg, although the name wasn't adopted until 1895.

The word "darg" means work – thus work done for love. It is believed to come from farming communities, which would frequently help one another out.

It soon developed into "A GRAND JUVENILE WILDFLOWER COMPETITION AND EXHIBITION" for the benefit of various sick children's hospitals.

In time it transformed into a major nationwide charitable appeal whereby readers would make thousands of gifts which were donated annually to over 80 hospitals, children's homes, care homes and hospices across the UK in time for Christmas.

There was a competition, too, with readers vying for prizes for the best entries in categories including babies, children's, toys and more.

Times changed and orphanages and asylums thankfully became a thing of the past. In the days of the automatic washing machine, it grew harder to find organisations and institutions happy to receive donations of knitted goods.

That is why, since 2010, "The People's Friend" has supported selected charities for each Love Darg appeal, asking for particular items or cash donations from readers. ■

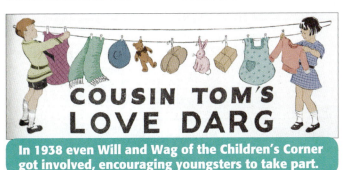

In 1938 even Will and Wag of the Children's Corner got involved, encouraging youngsters to take part.

During both World Wars the Love Darg was suspended while readers were urged to knit for the troops and refugees. Socks, gloves, balaclavas and scarves were frequently sent in. These would be parcelled up and sent to the Front.

Since beginning to work with specific charities, the Love Darg has supported the Red Cross, the Blue Cross, Age UK, Shelter and Cats Protection. Items knitted and crocheted include pet blankets and comforters, cat toys, tea cosies, hats, scarves, knee rugs and baby blankets.

New Century, New Monarch

Victoria's long reign was over, and a new King was on the throne. It was a time of change for the "Friend" and its loyal readers . . .

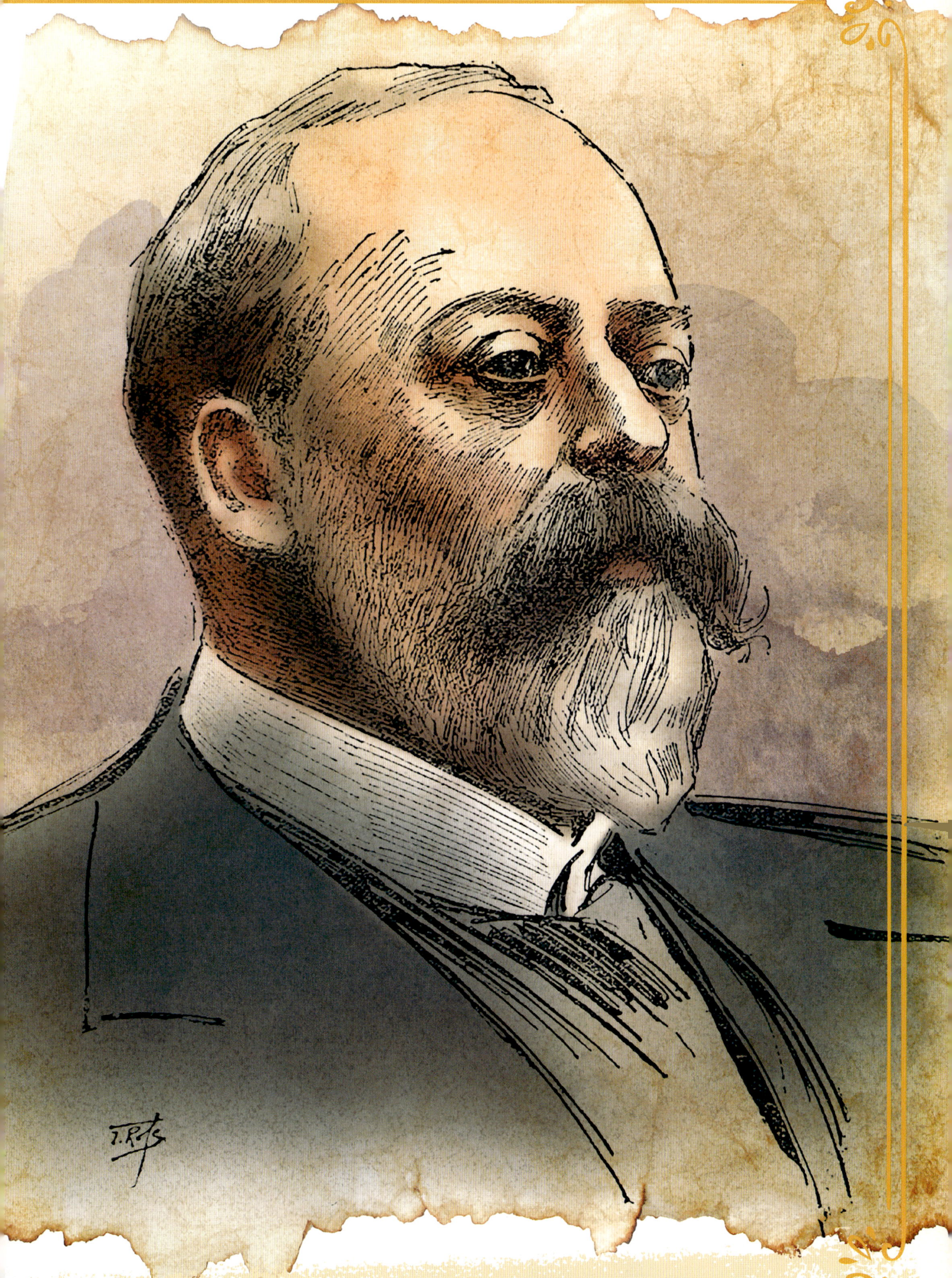

A New Era

With a new King came new optimism, and it seemed even the heavens were looking down kindly!

SADNESS after the death of Queen Victoria continued through the early months of 1901. The "Friend" published tributes and memories of the late Queen over many weeks.

However, the magazine also turned its thoughts to the future, and the accession of King Edward VII and Queen Alexandra. Special souvenir portraits were published. Anecdotes of the Royal couple brought them closer to their new subjects and there was intense interest in all aspects of the forthcoming coronation.

Interest wasn't confined to home matters, though. Correspondents from all over the globe brought news of world events. The "Friend" found cause for hope in 1901 in "Esperanto – A New International Language" that might bring people closer together. Later, there was a competition for written contributions in Esperanto. The winning entries were printed, too.

The race to the South Pole also merited attention.

"No less than four Antarctic expeditions are in course of preparation or under way!" the Editor reported excitedly in 1901, adding that RRS Discovery had already begun her voyage, and that she was "in every way worthy a national

> "No less than four Antarctic expeditions are in course of preparation or under way!" the Editor reported excitedly in 1901

enterprise and eminently creditable to Dundee, that famous birthplace of many a sturdy whaler and 'discoverer'. She will be commanded by Lieutenant R.F. Scott, R.N."

The same year brought news of the assassination in the United States of President McKinley, "Ruler And Martyr", as he was described.

The magazine was looking even farther afield in 1902 when it described to readers the recent discovery of Perseus, "the wonderful new star". Reproducing a photograph taken at the Yerkes Observatory in Chicago, the writer added, "The star is so wonderful and mysterious that even yet the astronomers have not quite made up their minds what to think about it."

Back on Earth, the staff were quite sure of what they thought about the latest conflict, the war in Tibet.

"As readers of newspapers must have noticed, we have embarked on another little war, which, however, like other expeditions of the sort, may turn out to be a much larger undertaking than was anticipated."

Perhaps most surprising is the speed with which the "Friend" reported on the 1905 Russian Revolution in St Petersburg. The gunning down of peaceful protestors in the city took place on January 22 (our calendar). In the February 6 issue, the magazine ran a feature on

1901-1905

Jan 1901

On January 22, after the death of his mother, Queen Victoria, Edward VII was proclaimed King.

Aug 1901

On August 30, English engineer Hubert Cecil Booth received a patent for the powered vacuum cleaner.

Dec 1901

The first Nobel Prizes were awarded in Stockholm. Named after Swedish inventor of dynamite Arthur Nobel, the awards were in recognition of men and women in the fields of physics, chemistry, physiology or medicine, literature and peace. The field of "Economic Sciences in Memory of Alfred Nobel" was established in 1968.

Aug 1902

On August 9, the coronation of Edward VII and Queen Alexandra took place in Westminster Abbey.

"St Petersburg, City Of Blood".

"We have heard of the streets of St Petersburg swimming in blood; of men, women, and children shot down by the brutal Cossack soldiery; of riot, rapine, and revolution in the capital city.

"There has been nothing like it in Europe since the streets of Paris echoed to the tumbrils of the Revolution . . . visitors to the capital, indeed, are always struck by the evidence of vast wealth on the one hand, and the most abject poverty on the other. So it was in Paris before the Revolution.

"And the fur-clad noble of St Petersburg, living his luxurious life, has only the Cossack soldiery between him and the fate that befell the French aristocrats," the writer stated prophetically.

Workers' lives at home were of interest, too. Throughout this period, the "Friend" profiled various industries, describing the operation of the factories and the occupations of the employees.

Readers received an account of "Cocoa And Chocolate: A Popular Industry"; "Bournville: Messrs Cadbury's Factory And Village" and "In Sweet-Land: All About The Making Of Confections" as well as heavier industries such as "In Wire-Land: How Cables And Wire-Nets Are Made", "In Rope-land: How Ropes Are Made" and "In Pottery-Land".

The accompanying illustrations give a fascinating insight into working life at the time – especially those depicting women at their posts.

Illustrations give a fascinating insight into working life at the time – especially those depicting women at their posts.

Life behind the scenes at the "Friend" was featured, too. Sir John Leng, M.P., celebrated his "journalistic jubilee" in 1901, giving the Editor the chance to tell readers more about their favourite magazine and how it was made. The "permanent enlargement of the 'People's Friend'" to "twenty-four pages and cover" afforded another such opportunity in 1903.

The "Friend" routinely encouraged working women – and it included working at home in that description, calling in 1903 for such work to be paid.

Outside the home, "The Work Of The Lady Journalist: An Interview With Miss Jane T. Stoddart" celebrated one of many women then making their name in public life, though advice for all was found every week.

"How To Become A Lady Chemist", "The Schoolmistress: Her Position And Prospects", "The Paisley Mill-Girls" and "Lady Helps And Servants" all described the varied lives of working women of the time.

In 1904 "Health Notes For Business Girls: A Talk To Typists, Clerks, Saleswomen And Others" bemoaned the fact that such women were neglecting their well-being through the perils of excessive tea-drinking, a poorly varied diet and a lack of adequate exercise. One of the remedies offered was "drink plenty of pure water". Some things never change! ■

Nov 1902

The popular toy name Teddy Bear was inspired by President Theodore "Teddy" Roosevelt on a hunting trip.

May 1903

On May 3, singer and actor Bing Crosby was born in Tacoma, Washington. The crooner merged a music and film career and appeared in the musical comedy "Road" series with co-stars Bob Hope and Dorothy Lamour. One of his greatest musical hits was "White Christmas".

Jan 1904

Motor vehicle registration and driver licences were required as part of the Motor Car Act of the previous year.

Sept 1905

Physicist Albert Einstein's paper on time and space was published, introducing the ground-breaking equation $E=mc^2$.

Long Live The King

By the end of the decade "Friend" readers found themselves no longer Edwardians, but instead entering a Georgian era.

IN the short years of Edward VII's reign great things would happen, and great events unfold. In 1908 the "Friend" marvelled at man's conquest of the skies by men such as the Wright brothers and Bleriot, and wondered who would first use and enjoy man's new power:

"Will it be the rich? Will it be the adventurous and the daring?"

In fact, France led the field, and was training up military men as aeronauts.

That same year came the news that Parliament had approved Old Age Pensions.

"The first day of the coming year marks the dawn of a new era for the old and the poor in the

That same year came the news that Parliament had approved Old Age Pensions

United Kingdom, for on that day something like half a million aged persons of both sexes will be entitled to a weekly

allowance from the Government, which, small though it may be, will at least keep hunger from

their doors and a roof over their heads for the balance of their days."

Readers were able to find out who was eligible, how

to claim, and how much they could receive.

Another important Act came into force in April of this year – the Children's Act, which would sweep away 22 old Acts and amend another 17.

One of the first clauses referred to "overlaying".

"By the new Act a tipsy or careless mother will find herself in a Court of Law to answer for her child's life should she suffocate in bed an infant below the age of three years."

Other clauses dealt with dangers from fire, particularly from an unprotected gate; the abolition of baby farms and

Farewell To Sausage

● The magazine staff experienced a sad loss with the demise of Sausage, the "Friend" dog.
This most sagacious canine in fact belonged to William C. Honeyman, the talented violinist and witty dispenser of pithy replies to the lovelorn, and

readers had been entertained for years with accounts of his exploits. "Sausage was more like a friend than a mere dog," Honeyman wrote, and dedicated a Strathspey and Reel to his dear companion who "clung to his master till the last."

1906-1910

April 1906

The Great San Francisco Earthquake caused fire and devastation, resulting in over 3000 fatalities.

Nov 1907

Florence Nightingale received the Order of Merit, Britain's highest civilian decoration. During the Crimean War, the "Lady with the Lamp", as she was affectionately referred to by the British soldiers, worked tirelessly as a nurse, improving the hygiene of military hospitals in Turkey.

Dec 1907

Rudyard Kipling, poet and author of "The Jungle Book", won the Nobel Prize for Literature.

April 1908

On April 5, "What Ever Happened To Baby Jane?" actress Bette Davis was born in Lowell, Massachusetts.

a ban on "tobacconists selling cigarettes to any boy who looks under 16."

"It is to be noted that only boys are dealt with in the Act. There is no word of girls. But it is usually long after that age that women take to tobacco; and one hardly, if ever, sees a gutter child sharing his cigarette with a sister."

A sombre note was reached in 1910 with the unexpected death of the monarch, King Edward the Peacemaker.

"The nation's memories of King Edward will ever be kindly and affectionate. He will stand out as a good man, as well as a good ruler."

Looking forward, as ever, the "Friend" welcomed a new King.

"King George the Fifth! Already we have taken kindly to the title.

"The Georgian days were days of adventure and romance, when smugglers abounded on our coasts, when if citizens did not sleep so soundly in their beds as they do now, there was a spice of adventure which has departed from our more prosaic days."

The Editor expressed his hope that the new Georgian era would be better than the old.

One thing which remained constant at this time was the column for would-be civil service correspondents.

This excellent scheme had already been running for over a decade, and there is no doubt that many a young man – and later, girl – achieved a place in their desired profession through the guidance of the "Friend".

Maladies

Within the pages of the "Friend" a reader could always find practical advice laced with good common-sense, as can be seen by this piece from 1908:

Approved Remedies For Every Day Maladies

For a fit of passion – Walk out in the open air. You may speak your mind to the winds without hurting anyone or proclaiming yourself a simpleton.

For a fit of idleness – Count the tickings of a clock. Do this for one hour and you will be glad to pull off your coat the next, and work hard.

For a fit of extravagance and folly – Go to the workhouse, or speak with the ragged inmates of a jail, and you will be convinced "Who makes his bed of briar and thorn, must be content to lie forlorn."

For a fit of ambition – Go into the churchyard and read the gravestones. They will tell you the end of ambition.

For a fit of repining – Look out for the halt and the blind, and visit the bedridden and afflicted and deranged, and they will make you ashamed of complaining of your lighter afflictions.

It was run by one William Thompson, who said:

"It is my fixed belief that there are many intelligent and industrious young men who are ignorant of the main facts that regulate the civil service, or who find out only when they are too old to take advantage of the opportunities they missed."

Under the old system, he attested, candidates were drawn from the younger sons of the upper classes.

"Who probably had no startling amount of book-learning but usually possessed an excellent physique and gentlemanly manners. And these, combined with skill in horsemanship, are for such a service as that of India perhaps quite as useful as a mere mass of undigested facts."

Thompson was set on focusing on different branches – Customs; Excise; Boy and Female Clerkships, among others.

What were the advantages of these?

"In the first place, everyone has an equal chance. No accident of birth stands in the way of success."

He prepared would-be candidates on proficiency in writing, spelling, arithmetic and composition. He also provided test papers of French for translation.

But the task before them would not be an easy one, as young people who took up the challenge were warned.

"I shall endeavour to set sure stepping-stones for willing feet, but if you know yourself to be of a flighty, fickle temperament think seriously before you begin."

July 1909

French aviator and inventor Louis Blériot became the first man to fly across the English Channel.

Nov 1909

The first Woolworths store opened in Liverpool's Church Street. American retailer F.W. Woolworth founded his store selling factory-made goods at affordable prices. During the 20th century, "Woolies" became one of the most recognisable retail names on British high streets, before its decline 100 years after it was established.

Aug 1910

On August 26, Catholic nun, missionary and humanitarian Mother Teresa was born in Skopje, Macedonia.

Oct 1910

E.M. Forster's "Howard's End" was published, a novel highlighting moral and social values at the turn of the century.

A World Of Change

With little sense that war clouds were building on the horizon, the "Friend" continued to play a central role in British households . . .

BY 1911, Britain was becoming familiar with its new King and Queen and eagerly anticipating their coronation. In February, the Editor announced an exciting competition, the winners of which would be privileged to join the staff in their Fleet Street offices to view the following day's Royal procession passing below the windows.

The magazine's 44th birthday was the next cause for celebration. Among the printed messages of congratulation was one from J.M. Barrie, author of "Peter Pan". Readers sent in their memories.

"It is now more than thirty years since I was first enthralled by 'People's Friend' stories," reader John Logan wrote. "In these earliest days I used to discuss the 'People's Friend' contents with a next door neighbour, a boy called Arthur Conan Doyle, now world-famous as the inventor of Sherlock Holmes."

Did some of those discussions concern the plots in the stories of one Detective James McGovan? These appeared in the pages of the "Friend" from 1873, penned by its very own "Violin Man", William Honeyman. What influence might they have had!

Attention moved to the wider world as the "Friend" observed at the opening of the Panama Canal that "The total amount of money spent in completing what has been described as the biggest job in the world will be about one hundred

1911-1914

June 1911
The Coronation of King George V, Queen's Victoria's grandson, and his consort, Queen Mary, took place in Westminster Abbey.

Jan 1912
Captain Robert Falcon Scott and his team completed their ill-fated mission to the South Pole.

April 1912
On April 12, the *Titanic* departed from Southampton en route to New York, but five days into her maiden voyage she sank after hitting an iceberg off the coast of Newfoundland, with the loss of over 1,500 lives.

July 1912
The modern pentathlon was first contested at the Olympic Games in Stockholm.

and sixty million pounds", an almost unimaginable sum at the time.

That year also saw the magazine reporting sadly on the loss of the *Titanic,* "The World's Greatest Ocean Tragedy", and considering the position of the women soldiers who had participated in China's Revolution.

Domestically, the national coal strike of 1912 led the magazine to discuss the role of alternative energy. It looked at "the coming of

"I used to discuss the 'People's Friend' contents with a next door neighbour, a boy called Arthur Conan Doyle"

oil", including vegetable oil alternatives, and a scheme to circumvent the mining industry by controlled combustion of underground coal seams to drive gas turbines, as well as "What The Wind Can Do: Windmills New And Old".

Readers were still given insights into the country's industry with portraits of the Lancashire cotton towns, including the child workers or "little nippers in the mills".

State-of-the-art food hygiene was described in a feature about the Brown & Polson cornflour factory in Paisley.

"The purity of the corn flour, not to mention the health of the girls themselves, is attended to by the taking of a bath at least once a week.

"For this purpose, a fine suite of bathrooms with attendants is provided, so that there is no need to wait for 'Sma' Shot Day' of the Fair holidays to indulge in a wash at the coast."

The Paisley workers seem to have been well looked after, with an early form of occupational pension and benefits scheme.

"When a beneficiary leaves, the full amount standing to his or her credit with all interest added is handed over.

"This is equal to a handsome 'tocher' to many a girl and may serve the way to square the obstacle to matrimonial prospects in Paisley suggested by the oft-repeated statement that there are seven girls to every man in the town."

This shortage of eligible males was revealed by the 1911 census, which had found there were 106.2 women for every 100 men in Scotland, where emigration was also resulting in the exodus of thousands (mostly men) every year.

It's clear, then, that many women had to be capable of supporting themselves.

Perhaps this explains why the magazine had such an emphasis on both business and domestic skills for women even before World War I changed things for ever. ■

The Modern Girl

Young ladies could look to their "Friend" for plenty of advice and guidance, though at times the Editor and his staff despaired of modern attitudes.

"The up-to-date girl is a stranger to the household machinery; a broom, duster or saucepan is never found in her hands." Lamenting the fact that to her "a crying baby is appalling", the writer continued, "she considers herself destined for some lofty mission in life. One day the housing of the poor occupies her attention exclusively; the next the subject of women's wages is rampant."

Education of girls was seen to be a mixed blessing. The modern girl, readers were told, "can talk French and German and write Latin and work out the stiffest problem old Euclid ever invented – BUT SHE CAN'T COOK!"

Could her ambitions lead ultimately to the scenes such as those in 1913; "the storming of the Houses of Parliament by the suffragettes, and the wild scenes witnessed in the vicinity of the Palace of Westminster"? Time would tell . . .

Aug 1912

On August 23, actor, dancer and "Singin' In The Rain" star Gene Kelly was born in Pittsburgh.

April 1913

"The Cat And Mouse Act" was rushed through Parliament, allowing the temporary discharge of prisoners due to ill health. This came about as a result of hunger strikes by suffragettes, who were in danger of starvation. Once their health had recovered, the suffragettes were recalled to prison.

Aug 1913

Inspired by Hans Christian Andersen's Mermaid tale, the Little Mermaid statue was unveiled in Copenhagen.

Jan 1914

On January 5, actor George Reeves, who played television's Superman in the 1950s, was born in Woolstock, Iowa.

On The Cover

A new century, and at the age of thirty the "Friend" could no longer be regarded a mere stripling . . .

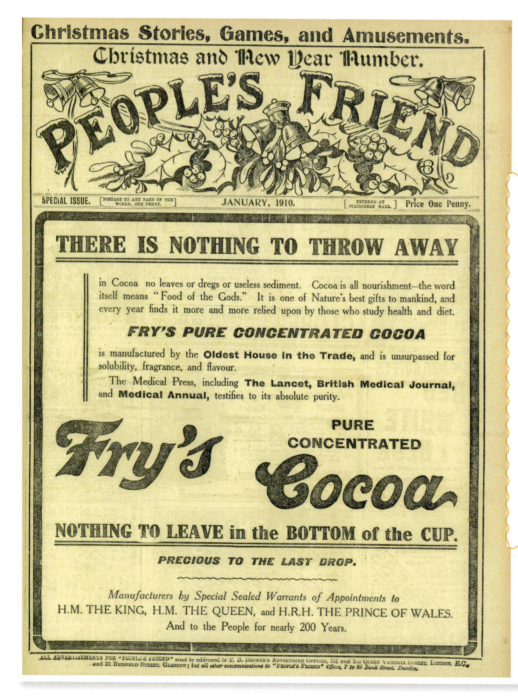

Christmas Stories, Games, and Amusements.

Christmas and New Year Number.

PEOPLE'S FRIEND

SPECIAL ISSUE. [POSTAGE TO ANY PART OF THE WORLD, ONE PENNY.] JANUARY, 1910. [ENTERED AT STATIONERS' HALL.] Price One Penny.

THERE IS NOTHING TO THROW AWAY

in Cocoa no leaves or dregs or useless sediment. Cocoa is all nourishment—the word itself means "Food of the Gods." It is one of Nature's best gifts to mankind, and every year finds it more and more relied upon by those who study health and diet.

FRY'S PURE CONCENTRATED COCOA

is manufactured by the **Oldest House in the Trade**, and is unsurpassed for solubility, fragrance, and flavour.

The Medical Press, including **The Lancet, British Medical Journal,** and **Medical Annual**, testifies to its absolute purity.

Fry's PURE CONCENTRATED *Cocoa*

NOTHING TO LEAVE in the BOTTOM of the CUP.

PRECIOUS TO THE LAST DROP.

Manufacturers by Special Sealed Warrants of Appointments to
H.M. THE KING, H.M. THE QUEEN, and H.R.H. THE PRINCE OF WALES.
And to the People for nearly 200 Years.

ALL ADVERTISEMENTS FOR "PEOPLE'S FRIEND" must be addressed to T. B. BROWNE'S ADVERTISING OFFICES, 161 and 163 QUEEN VICTORIA STREET, LONDON, E.C., and 22 RENFIELD STREET, GLASGOW; but all other communications to "PEOPLE'S FRIEND" Offices, 7 to 25 Bank Street, Dundee.

January 1910

The next five years would see not one but two Kings on the throne. The death of Edward VII would bring together Europe's royalty, many of whom were his relations, for the last time before the assassination of an archduke in Sarajevo. Edward was succeeded by his son, George V. Meanwhile, the "Friend" thrived . . .

Nov 11, 1901

What the well-dressed matron was wearing.

Jan 4, 1904

This serial was already on its 28th weekly instalment!

Oct 11, 1909

The "Friend" is now "The Favourite Home Journal".

Aug 8, 1910

War waged against the disease-carrying house-fly.

From the very first issue, the Editor has been the bridge between the "Friend" and its readers.

Your Editor

Since the magazine's launch 150 years ago, only a handful of people have been lucky enough to sit in the "Friend" Editor's chair.

SINCE the very first issue, the figure of the Editor has been central to the "Friend". His was the voice that articulated the magazine's founding statement in January 13, 1869, and it was he who communicated any new developments or innovations to the reader at regular intervals. He was the bridge between the magazine's staff and its readers – and, in print at least, he was completely anonymous.

Down through the years, the Editor was never named or pictured within the title's pages. It was a tradition typical of the ethos of the magazine; it was the "Friend" itself that was the star, not any one person who worked on it.

And not identifying the Editor – and thus then not having to introduce a new person when the previous incumbent left – gave continuity and a sense of never-changing timelessness to the magazine.

It wasn't until 2012 that the Editor's name and picture became a feature of each issue, in response to the expectations of a modern audience.

Records exist of all the people who have served as Editor of "The People's Friend, with one exception. Mystery surrounds the identity of the Editor between 1938 and 1945. There are mentions of John B. Davidson as Editor-in-Chief of Magazines at the time, but no specific reference to an Editor of the "Friend".

It is not unreasonable to suppose that, during World War II, the need to keep going through turbulent times and with limited resources took precedence over the luxury of having an editor dedicated to one title.

The "Friend" launched in January 1869 under the stewardship of Tammas Bodkin, the pen-name of W.D. Latto, who was the Editor of "The People's Journal".

He was a remarkable man who had risen from humble beginnings as a handloom weaver in the Fife village of Ceres to become a teacher, journalist and writer, and then an editor.

He was an ardent supporter of the Scots language and was one of the pioneers of the "Kailyard School" of Scottish literature.

He was also universally popular and well liked.

"It is an excellent thing to have a sunny disposition," John Leng said of him, "and Mr Latto, while thoroughly genuine and sincere, takes the sunshine with him wherever he goes."

When it became clear the new publication was a success, a full-time editor was required, and David Pae took on the role.

Born in Perthshire in 1828, he was an accomplished writer as well as an experienced editor, and was a prolific creator

Tammas Bodkin was the pen-name of William D. Latto.

of serialised fiction. In 1863 he began contributing to "The People's Journal", which led to him moving to Newport in Fife, just across the Tay from Dundee.

In tandem with his second-in-command Andrew Stewart, David Pae took the "Friend" from strength to strength.

At least three of his own serial stories were published in the magazine

When it became clear the new publication was a success, a full-time Editor was required, and David Pae took on the role

– "Norah Cushaleen", "Nelly Preston" and "The Captain's Bride".

He was a modest man, and few realised just how prolific a writer he was. At his funeral, the minister said, "It will be very difficult to know everything he wrote, for to not a single production from his pen did he put his name."

He was an active churchgoer and was noted for his "amiability and gentleness".

"His aim throughout all his romances was to please, to amuse, to thrill, to excite; but it was also to instruct, to elevate, to humanise," the "Dundee Advertiser" reported.

David Pae died suddenly on May 9, 1884, aged fifty-six. It was said he had been working in his garden just the evening before, having spent the day on a new novel to appear in "The People's Journal".

He was succeeded in the Editor's chair by his colleague and sub-editor Andrew Stewart, who was born in Glasgow in 1842.

In 1893, Andrew Stewart celebrated his "semi Jubilee" as Editor with a function at Darling's Regent Hotel in Edinburgh, at which he was presented with his portrait.

Colleagues and contributors were invited, and the party numbered around 100.

Andrew Stewart was a prolific writer of fiction, poetry and music, and for many years he was also the music critic of "The Evening Telegraph". He specialised in "fine, human and wholesome works of fiction, infused with tenderness."

He was held in high regard by colleagues, contributors and friends: "He simply bristled with honesty . . . His influence was ever on the side of the good, the beautiful, and the true."

When Andrew Stewart died suddenly on his way to the office in 1900, the Editorship was taken up by David Pae junior, son of the first Editor.

He was to go on to be the longest-serving Editor of all, clocking up an amazing 38 years, and

A Self-made Man

From humble beginnings in a religious home in Glasgow, Andrew Stewart rose to become an esteemed writer and journalist. He was very much a self-made man, an avid reader who attended "improvement" classes at the Spoutmouth Bible Institute as a youngster.

He started his working life as a "feeder" in the paper-ruling works in Glasgow run by Messrs Lumsden.

He contributed regularly to the first few issues of the "Friend" and was "invited to become sub-editor" before the magazine was a year old.

He had a sound training under the first David Pae, and his obituary noted, "Very faithfully and brilliantly did he carry out the sure policy and high principle laid down by his predecessor."

After his sudden death, the Dundee "Evening Telegraph" printed a poetic tribute from the Roper Bard:

"A precious light gone out in to shine no more;

"Such lights are scarce where they are needed most."

more than any other person, he shaped the character and direction of the "Friend".

He was also an accomplished author in his own right who, under the name Ian Farquhar, created a series of popular and amusing stories set in the fictional village of Pickletillie.

In January 1938, "The Courier And Advertiser" reported on the "Journalistic Jubilee of Mr David Pae", a dinner in the Royal Hotel in Dundee attended by 180 people, at which he was presented with a service of silver plate.

A tribute from Mr D.C. Thomson was read out in which he stated simply, "The 'Friend' is David Pae,

and David Pae is the 'Friend'."

In a toast at the dinner, it was noted that "'The People's Friend' has been his lifework. He has, in truth, lived for his paper and its readers."

Annie S. Swan added her own appreciation: "To him I owe my long association with 'The People's Friend', which I regard as the brightest jewel in my small earthly crown."

In reply, recalling that as a boy he used to read manuscripts that his father brought home from the office, David Pae said that "love of the 'Friend' had been in his blood from his earliest years, and he had watched over it with the greatest joy and satisfaction." ◼

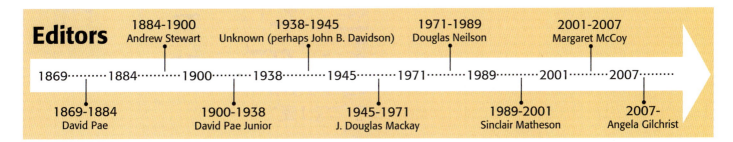

Editors

1869 ········ 1884 ········ 1900 ········ 1938 ········ 1945 ········ 1971 ········ 1989 ········ 2001 ········ 2007 ········

1884-1900 Andrew Stewart
1938-1945 Unknown (perhaps John B. Davidson)
1971-1989 Douglas Neilson
2001-2007 Margaret McCoy

1869-1884 David Pae
1900-1938 David Pae Junior
1945-1971 J. Douglas Mackay
1989-2001 Sinclair Matheson
2007- Angela Gilchrist

Song And Dance

"Friend" readers would have found their feet tapping with these musical offerings!

WHEN the "Friend" appeared in 1869 it was to a very different world. In this media-saturated age we move about our daily life surrounded by music. Whether introducing news items, advertising goods, enticing customers into shops, or enjoying our own playlists through those little earbuds, we have become accustomed to this background accompaniment.

Those first "Friend" readers would certainly have been just as fond of music and entertainment, but with no TV, no internet and no radio, they had to look elsewhere.

This was the golden age of music halls, and concertgoers would enjoy hearing the popular songs on the stage. They would then go home to reproduce them on the piano, which had become a symbol of social status, on the violin or simply by singing them.

With this background, it is easy to see why the "Friend" began, almost from the first, to incorporate songsheets into its pages.

Gradually these took the form of songbooks, offered free with the issue, so that even up to the 1960s readers could sing or play along with well-loved tunes.

TV celebrities had appeared by now, with Andy Stewart, Kenneth McKellar and the Alexander Brothers all firm favourites both within Scotland and beyond.

Eventually the musical gifts evolved into Christmas cassettes of carols, and then CDs, which continue to the present day. ■

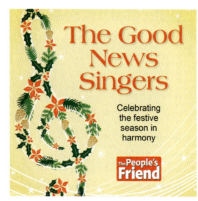

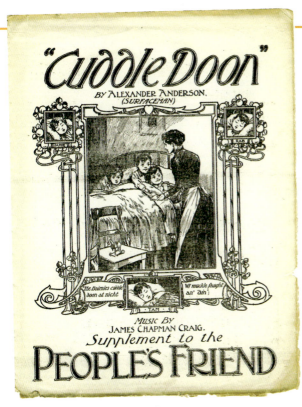

Surfaceman

One early contributor was poet Alexander Anderson, also known as "Surfaceman".

Born in Kirkconnel, Dumfries and Galloway, at sixteen he was working in a quarry and then became a surfaceman or platelayer on the Glasgow and South-western railway. This was the name he wrote under.

In 1870 he began to send verses to the magazine, and his first book, "A Song Of Labour And Other Poems", sold out within a fortnight. He was aided by the support of the Rev. George Gilfillan, a poetry critic

in Dundee. His most fondly remembered poem was "Cuddle Doon", a sentimental ballad followed by "Wauken Up", and then "The Last To Cuddle Doon".

Cuddle Doon

The bairnies cuddle doon at nicht
Wi muckle faught and din.
"Oh, try an' sleep, ye waukrife rogues,
Your faither's comin' in."
They niver heed a word I speak,
I try tae gie a froon,
But aye I hap them up an' cry
"Oh, bairnies, cuddle doon!"

Wee Jamie wi' the curly heid,
He aye sleeps next the wa'
Bangs up and cries, "I want a piece!"
The rascal starts them a'.
I rin and fetch them pieces, drinks,
They stop a wee the soun',
Then draw the blankets up an' cry,
"Noo, weanies, cuddle doon."

But ere five minutes gang, wee Rab
Cries oot frae neath the claes,
"Mither, mak' Tam gie ower at aince,
He's kittlin' wi' his taes."
The mischief in that Tam for tricks,
He'd bother half the toon,
But aye I hap them up an' cry,
"Oh, bairnies, cuddle doon!"

At length they hear their faither's fit
An' as he steeks the door,
They turn their faces tae the wa'
An Tam pretends tae snore.
"Hae a' the weans been gude?" he asks,
As he pits aff his shoon.
"The bairnies, John, are in their beds
An' lang since cuddled doon!"

An' just afore we bed oorsel's
We look at oor wee lambs,
Tam has his airm roun' wee Rab's neck
An Rab his airm roun' Tam's.
I lift wee Jamie up the bed
An' as I straik each croon,
I whisper till my heart fills up:
"Oh, bairnies, cuddle doon!"

The bairnies cuddle doon at nicht
Wi' mirth that's dear tae me.
But soon the big warl's cark an' care
Will quaten doon their glee.
Yet come what will to ilka ane,
May He who rules aboon,
Aye whisper, though their pows be bald:
"Oh, bairnies, cuddle doon!"

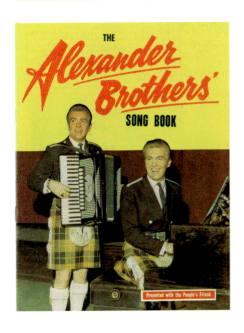

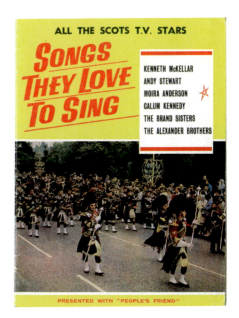

Working men and women dreamed of being published poets and writers.

Poetry Of The People

The young magazine prided itself on a high standard of verse, especially from its readers . . .

THE Victorian era was the heyday of newspaper poetry, and the "Friend", like its sister paper "The People's Journal", contained a large and varied selection of verse in every issue.

Poems were not simply fillers used to pad out short columns; they were an integral part of the "Friend" and covered a range of topics, from sentimental lines about family members and romantic verses to loved ones to biting satire and political commentary.

Importantly, readers from all backgrounds, and especially the working classes, were encouraged to submit their poems.

In the first issue in 1869, the Editor set out his position: "Believing that the thirst for literary distinction amongst the labouring classes is a feeling which ought to be cultivated, as tending to promote self-improvement and studious, sober habits, we shall have pleasure in opening the columns of the 'Friend' to the contributions of the people."

For the lucky few who saw their work in print, the satisfaction of having proof that they were capable of more than a lifetime of drudgery must have been immense. For the rest, there was the opportunity to receive advice and criticism – though this was sometimes scathing – through the "To Correspondents" column.

Victorian Scotland prided itself on being a literary nation, home of Robert Burns, and both "Friend" and "Journal" actively promoted the use of the Scots language, which would-be poets, readers and editorial staff alike valued for its richness of expression and capacity for humour.

My Highland Home (1869)

Away, far away,
Over mountains gray,
Is my Highland home,
Where my heart will stray,
Where the torrents foam
And the wild deer roam
O'er the hills and dales
Of my Highland home.
In a wooded dell,
Where the azure bell
Deckt the smiling banks,
Where a cascade fell,
'Neath an oak's green
  dome,
Bounded by the foam
Of the rushing stream
Is my Highland home.
  J.B.P., Glasgow.

A Mither's Blether About Her Bairn (1869)

That bairn o' mine'll drive me daft,
I solemnly declare;
If I had bedlam in the house
It couldna plague me mair.
He waukens up by screigh o' day
Then rest wi' him there's nane,
But rumbling', tumblin' up and doon –
It's no' a common wean!
He's never oot o' mischief, an'
He never seems to tire.
See! There he's on the fender edge –
He'll tumble in the fire.
He's at the door noo – catch him or
He'll tumble doon the stair;
He's got the puir cat – how the smout
Is ruggin' out its hair.
Losh! Noo he's got his father's book
Wide open on his knee;
And just observe the solemn look
That's in his bonny e'e.
He canna read, yet looks as grave
As chiel' in gown or band;
But mair than he look grave on things
They dinna understan'.
An unco wean; yet flyte on him,
He only laughs and craws
Like his father when he's teasing me;
Or when I tak' the tawse
An' gie'm a skelp, I'm vexed, an' wish
I'd let the bairn alane,
For he looks sae strange-like in my face,
I couldna do't again.

J.W.T., Earlsferry.

In Memoriam (1873)

John Bell, late Contributor to the Friend.

Few were his years, but bright as brief –
This world to him no place of gloom,
Through which poor mortals, bowed with grief,
Must travel trembling to the tomb.
With manly heart and genial smile
Along life's rugged path he trod,
Amongst the lowly sons of toil,
With faith in man and hope in God.
No laggard he to linger last,
Content while struggling in the rear,
But boldly, bravely pressing past
The shrinking crowd kept back through fear.
He hoped to win a name and place
Amongst that highly-honoured band,
Whose works and thoughts and sayings grace
The annals of our favoured land.
Alas! That hopes so brave and bright,
Like summer flowers should withered lie –
That weak ones should be left to fight
Life's battle while the bravest die.

J.K.C.

To the Editor of "The People's Friend" (1894)

I want a wife that's guid and true,
To bake, and wash, and darn, and sew,
Keep a'thing tidy, clean and neat
On less than thirty shillings a week.
When well, of course, she will require
To black the boots and light the fire,
To mak' the parritch, mask the tea,
And aye be in the best o' glee.
Yet one thing more I must demand –
I want her heart as well's her hand,
To cheer me on life's rugged way
And chase foreboding cares away.
And as for age, say, let her be
From eighteen to twenty-three;
For height in stockings, shoes complete,
A little under quite six feet.

A.G.

To Correspondents

● And so you think that "if we only knew the darling the poem is all about, we would order it to be set up in special type."
A perusal of the poem reconciles us to the fact we don't know her. We can, however, promise it a specially good place in the waste basket, where it will serve the purpose of warming the editorial toes when the fire is made up.

● The piece is too long, and it only tells in narrative rhyme a story that is familiar in prose.

● JSS waxes wroth at us because his poem was not inserted.
"I insist on its insertion next week. If you had a few grain of sense and literary skill you would have had my verses in."
Here is a verse from said poem:
Roll on, thou rushing, roaring brook,
Yet tarry ye a while,
And on dear nature take a look
As on your way you toil,
But no, in angry flood you rush
O'er dams and falls you flee,
As anxious for the final plash
To vanish in the sea.

World At War

When Britain declared war on Germany on August 4, 1914, almost overnight the "Friend", like the women who loved to read it, was plunged into a new and challenging role in a fast-changing world.

Russian Gingerbread

(1916)

- ½ lb. flour
- 2 oz. sugar
- ½ teaspoonful soda
- ½ teaspoonful ground cloves
- ½ teaspoonful mixed spice
- ¼ teaspoonful ground ginger
- 3 oz. margarine
- 2 oz. ginger chips
- 1 oz. almonds
- 2 tablespoonsful syrup
- 1 egg
- Pinch of salt, and milk to mix

Rub margarine into the flour, then add soda, sugar, and spices, ginger chips cut into dice, the syrup, egg well beaten, and milk to make it a soft consistency; beat until smooth. Pour into greased and floured cake tin, sprinkle the almonds, which have been blanched and shredded, on the top, and bake in a slow oven 40 to 45 minutes.

Love And Sacrifice

While their men went off to fight, the women who were left behind had to find the strength to carry on.

IN August 1914, everything changed almost overnight, and with change came suffering. The men who had been the sole wage-earners for their families were gone; many others found themselves unemployed as their jobs were swept away by the need to focus on making weapons and military equipment.

It wasn't long before many families in Britain found themselves in want, and as a result, one of the first wartime appeals in the "Friend" was not, as might be expected, for socks and mitts for the soldiers, but a heartfelt plea for clothes for the Relief Fund at home.

Before long, everyone's lives were transformed, and the "Friend" exhorted its readers not to panic, but to carry on as normal, declaring it was every man's duty to go off to fight, and every woman's duty to assist that effort.

Her part might be to take over a man's job to free him up to fight, work in one of the munitions factories, or help grow and harvest desperately needed food. Above all, she must ensure that morale was held high – and the "Friend" made it its mission to help her in

The work of the women for our soldiers comes like a gleam of sunshine in a dark and stormy sky

that aim: "In time of trouble we all need distraction and cheer, and that is what the 'Friend' offers you, and will continue to offer you. To read the 'Friend' as usual is one of the best resolutions you can make."

Its pages rapidly filled with accounts of war work from every field.

"The work of the women for our soldiers comes like a gleam of sunshine in a dark and stormy sky, reminding us that love and self-sacrifice still exist in a world of strife and hatred."

The war soon made its impact felt on the content of the magazine. Advertisements were aimed at working girls, and fashions became more practical. Short stories with titles such as "At The Front" (Adventures Of Nurse Laura Of The Red Cross) and "Mary Masterman, Munition Mistress" began to appear, and suddenly, how to use up scraps was a necessity for the cook!

Kitty, the cookery editor, addressed her "dear housewives" shortly after the outbreak of war: "I am sure you are all feeling the shoe already beginning to

---

1914-1915

Feb 1914

In February, Charlie Chaplin made his film debut in the short comedy "Making A Living".

June 1914

English author Laurie Lee, best known for his memoir "Cider With Rosie", was born in Stroud, Gloucestershire.

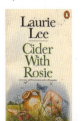

June 1914

On June 28, the assassination of Archduke Franz Ferdinand of Austria and his wife, Duchess Sophie, in Sarajevo set in motion the events that led to the outbreak of World War I. The heir presumptive to the Austro-Hungarian throne was shot by nineteen-year-old Serbian Gavrilo Princip.

July 1914

The Royal Naval Air Service, fore-runner of the Royal Air Force, was established.

A British Hydroplane during World War I.

pinch . . . I have drawn up a number of dishes as economically as I can, and I am sure you will find the recipes useful in this time of stress."

Kitty's recipes included Ox Foot Broth, Liver Soup and Two Days' Dinner From A Sheep's Pluck.

"This is a serious time for us all," she wrote, "but we can only hope that the dark cloud may soon show its silver lining."

By the end of November 1914, wounded soldiers were already returning from the Front, and the need for nourishing recipes to aid recovery was clear.

"I thought a page of invalid cookery would be welcome," Kitty wrote. She recommended Carrageen Blanc Mange, carrageen being an Irish moss believed to have healing properties.

Even though thrift was now the watchword of every housewife, treats were much appreciated and hearts were generous.

Readers made goodies to fill hampers for Tommy and sent in hundreds of cakes and sweetmeats in response to Kitty's "Cakes And Candy Competition" to raise funds for a YMCA hut for the troops.

And it wasn't just edible gifts that were supplied. Through the magazine's Help One Another Club, staff member Eleanor urged women to make sure troops had plenty of warm clothing: "My Dear Sisters – I am extremely grateful for the way in which you have all responded to my appeal for garments and woollen comforts for the soldiers . . .

"But although we have

Short stories such as "At The Front" (Adventures Of Nurse Laura Of The Red Cross) reflected women's changing roles.

done so well already we must persist in our labours, for no woollies will last for ever. Let 'ever doing' be our watchwords and your men will bless us."

To assist the women in making the items most needed, the "Friend" regularly printed patterns and instructions for socks, mufflers and waistcoats, caps to wear with steel helmets, and a range of gloves and mittens for specific uses.

The knitted rifle glove featured an open thumb and forefinger to allow use of the rifle, and the Mellor Glove for minesweepers was like a huge oven glove but with the top cut away and a flap fitted.

There were many appeals in the "Friend" over the war years, but one of the most touching was launched by Eleanor in 1915, asking readers to help Belgian babies.

The Belgian refugee crisis

of World War I was the largest refugee movement in British history, with hundreds of thousands fleeing Belgium when the Germans invaded.

"I wish I could describe to you what mothers are suffering owing to not having the wherewithal to feed and clothe their little ones," Eleanor wrote, and "Friend" readers gave generously, even though they had little enough to spare. ■

August 1914

On August 4, Britain declared war on Germany following the invasion of neutral Belgium.

August 1914

The first electric traffic light was installed on the corner of Euclid Avenue and East 105th Street in Cleveland, USA.

May 1915

On May 7, the British ocean liner *RMS Lusitania* was sunk by a German U-boat off the south-west coast of Ireland. The tragedy resulted in the deaths of 1,198 civilians who were travelling from New York to Liverpool and played a significant part in turning public opinion in the US against Germany.

Sept 1915

The Women's Institute was founded to encourage women to help produce food during the war.

theWI
INSPIRING WOMEN

Make Do And Mend

Thrift, ingenuity and generosity – these were the values the magazine encouraged its readers to show as war raged on.

AS the war wore on, the "Friend" devoted more and more pages to thrift and "make do and mend". Hints and advice varied from the useful to the bizarre!

The thrifty matron hoping to restore a worn serge suit was advised to "sponge it with hot vinegar and press on the wrong side with a warm iron", while readers in possession of an old skirt were assured that it might be "cut up and transformed into a most serviceable pair of knickers."

The consequences of war were felt even in the world of fashion.

In 1914, dresses were still heavily influenced by the Edwardian era, with long narrow skirts and tight corsetry in vogue, but by 1915 women were already moving away from such restrictive outfits. Skirts became shorter and fuller, and fabrics were chosen for their durability and practicality.

Paper patterns in the "Friend" quickly began to reflect these changes: "Just recently there has been an exceptional demand for patterns for the many utility garments worn by the great army of our women war workers to-day."

Military influences also became apparent as the war progressed, with the trench coat, sailor-style blouses and Cossack-style hats all popular choices.

When not stitching, hardworking readers were knitting, crocheting and patching clothes, running a household and in many cases taking on a job outside the home.

All that and ensuring

When not stitching, hardworking readers were knitting, crocheting and patching clothes

their children were cared for, too.

The war was a tough and terrifying time for youngsters, and the

Inspiration For The Home Milliner

Being at war was no excuse for leaving home without suitable headgear! As the war progressed, large-brimmed hats gave way to simpler styles such as the sailor hat and cloche, and even the turban. Sadly, the veiled hat also became a common sight, with widows and bereaved mothers adding a black veil to denote mourning.

1915-1917

Sept 1915
Cecil Chubb bought Stonehenge at auction for £6,600. Three years later, he gifted the site to the nation.

Sept 1915
The two-week-long Battle of Loos, the biggest British attack of 1915, began. It was the first occasion on which Britain used poison gas as a weapon of war. British forces took the French town of Loos, but significant casualties were incurred.

March 1916
Harold Wilson, future Prime Minister of the UK, was born in Huddersfield, Yorkshire.

July 1916
The Battle of the Somme, one of the bloodiest of the war, began in northern France. It lasted for 140 days. More than three million men fought in it, and there were over one million casualties from both sides. The huge death toll shocked the world and brought home the horror of the war to many people in the UK in a way that earlier battles had not.

"Friend" did its best to keep up their morale.

One thing the magazine didn't do was shelter youngsters from the reality of the war; a rather gruesome story called "Sir Guy And The Sausages" featured a machine that ground up a German giant to make sausages, and a game entitled "Pot Shots At The Kaiser" came with this instruction for young readers: "Every patriotic boy or girl will see to it that they are aiming at the Kaiser!"

For the women left behind at home while their men went off to fight, the "Friend" was a source of advice, information and comfort, and on the magazine's letters page, they found a friend in Uncle Jack, who dispensed patriotic sympathy and words of wisdom along with boxes of tea.

The magazine even provided advice for the lovelorn parted by the war in the column "Love Knots Untied".

Written by staff member William C. Honeyman, the column had little patience with selfish girls and fickle men; the acerbic advice given must have jolted many a lovesick reader back to her senses.

"The fact that your lover bears a resemblance to the wretched Crown Prince should not set you against him, but that he is a coward is fatal.

"You are right to despise him, and you should put him entirely out of your mind."

It wasn't long before wartime shortages began to affect the "Friend".

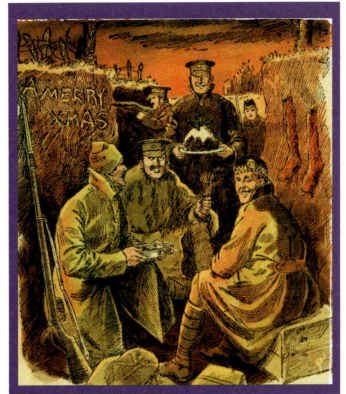

Christmas In The Trenches

At no time was the absence of loved ones felt more acutely than at Christmas. The "Friend" did its best to bring cheer during those dark days with encouragement from Uncle Jack, party games from Cousin Tom, and recipes from the ever-resourceful Kitty.

By Christmas 1915 the "Friend" had a number of contributors with direct experience of serving at the Front, and was able to paint an accurate picture of how loved ones overseas might be spending their Christmas, with articles such as "Christmas Eve In a Dug-Out" describing soldiers sheltering "six feet under the skin of the earth, with a floor area of 4 yards by 3."

And yet even in such unpromising surroundings, the men had decorated with "some rough and ready festoons, fashioned out of tinted odds and ends", which lent "a convivial air to things."

In 1917, the magazine summed up the feelings of many: "So a war-time Christmas is here again; Christmas and the guns still firing, Christmas and the bombs still exploding! But let us be of good cheer. Christmas and all it stands for is still with us. The dear Christmas rites will survive long after the war has been forgotten. Peace and Good Will are the eternal, the abiding things."

By February 1916, paper was in short supply, leading to a reduction in numbers printed, and it also became harder to send magazines to loved ones overseas.

The bound volume for 1917 is noticeably slimmer than its counterparts from the earlier war years, and the reason is simple. By March of that year, paper shortages were biting so badly that the magazine had to be reduced in size.

The Editor, though, refused to be downhearted, and in 1917 declared: "I am glad to say that through all this storm and stress the 'Friend' has held up well; indeed, it seems to be more firmly rooted than ever in the warm affection of a large and ever-increasing circle."

The women of Britain, too, were expected to hold up well, and many did, relishing the opportunity to escape the restrictions of domesticity and embracing their new-found freedom.

They took on work as drivers, railway officials and munitions workers, posties, bank clerks and construction workers; over the course of the war 600,000 women took on previously male-dominated roles in industry.

"Our taxi girl in our new series is a bright, clever, spirited, resourceful lass, as you will see from her account of her adventures," the Editor wrote.

"War work is evolving new types of female characters, what with tram-drivers and conductors, female railway servants and motor drivers, to say nothing of the many other things women are doing nowadays." ∎

Jan 1917

American frontiersman and showman William F. "Buffalo Bill" Cody died aged 70.

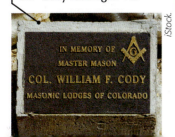

April 1917

Under the leadership of President Woodrow Wilson, the United States declared war on Germany.

iStock

July 1917

The Cottingley Fairies photos were taken in Yorkshire. It wasn't until 1981 that the two cousins involved, Elsie Wright and Frances Griffiths, admitted to faking the images.

July 1917

King George V issued a proclamation stating that, in future, the Royal Family would bear the surname Windsor.

Rex

> **The soldiers were coming home, bringing with them fresh winds of change.**

Peace At Last

The war was nearing an end, but would things ever be the same again?

AS the months and years wore on, food became increasingly scarce. By January 1917, there was talk of a potato famine, and by March certain items such as tea, coffee and cocoa had been prohibited as imports. Flour and sugar were in short supply, and expensive. More than ever, Kitty's sage advice was required, and she rose magnificently to the challenge, even coming up with a recipe for sugarless jam.

Meatless days were now a feature in all households, and with meat rationed and fuel soaring in price, recipes and tips to keep down the butcher's bill and save coal and gas were in demand. Kitty sought the help of an expert, Mrs J.S. of Newport, Fife, who extolled the virtues of hay-box cookery: "I was asked recently what the hay box would cook, and I replied – 'Anything, with the exception of steamed puddings.'"

1917-1918

Aug 1917
Actor Robert Mitchum was born in Bridgeport, Connecticut.

Aug 1917
War poets Wilfred Owen and Siegfried Sassoon met whilst convalescing at Craiglockhart War Hospital, Edinburgh.

November 1917
The People's Dispensary for Sick Animals was founded in London by Maria Dickin to provide care for sick and injured animals belonging to the poor. It went on to become the UK's leading pet wellbeing charity.

January 1918
National sugar rationing was introduced as shortages caused by the German U-boat campaign began to bite. People in the UK were allowed half a pound of this prized commodity per week.

Such ingenuity and generosity was typical of the "Friend" and its readers throughout the war. The demonstration of both thrift and generosity to others, in the sharing of recipes, tips and foodstuffs, was a hallmark of Kitty's cookery column during that period, and although the end of the war brought a welcome peace, it did not bring a return to the pre-war days of comparative plenty.

The enormous price rises in basic foodstuffs and fuel left many families struggling to make ends meet, and Kitty and her Kitchen Club continued to dispense valuable advice.

What might happen "after the war" was a topic the "Friend" gave much thought to, pondering how its female readers would adapt to quieter times – and how men might react to the modern, independent women they came home to.

"Many of them will quietly and contentedly take up their household duties again, but not a few will desire to go out into the world and seek employment."

Did that happen? Probably not. Knowing the grit, courage and determination of "Friend" readers both then and now, it's doubtful they were quite so compliant about their return to domesticity!

As November 1918 approached, the realisation that the war might finally be nearing an end drew an outpouring of relief and joy from the Editor.

"Peace may be here sooner than we think, who knows, and we may be ushered into the after-war

Knowing the grit, courage and determination of "Friend" readers both then and now, it's doubtful they were quite so compliant about their return to domesticity!

period to which we are all looking forward.

"What will it be like to live in a world where the latest war news will not be the absorbing thing every morning and afternoon?

"I am, of course, longing for the day when the present restrictions will be removed, and I shall be able to present you with a bigger and, I hope, a better 'People's Friend'."

Magazine lead-times being what they were, it was not until the issue dated November 23, 1918, that the end of the war could finally be acknowledged. Restrictions, though, would continue for the foreseeable future: "Though the war is happily over, the scarcity of paper, among other things, still continues, and I fear we shall not be back to our old conditions for a considerable time." ■

Animal Heroes

Long before "War Horse" reminded us of the role animals played during World War I, the "Friend" was keeping its readers informed of how vital animals of all kinds were to the war effort.

In 1915, it reported that "Our enemies have also made use of carrier pigeons, not merely for conveying messages, but for taking military photographs," while "Dogs At the Front" in 1916 described how dogs were used for patrol and sentry work, for helping the stretcher-bearers find wounded men, and even for drawing machine guns. Dogs were also used for conveying crucial communications between soldiers.

Perhaps the greatest bond was between soliders and their horses. The devotion went two ways, and the "Friend" reported many stories of the body of a fallen man being guarded by his four-legged companion.

"The horse itself was unharmed. Later on some of our men very bravely arranged to get out to the horse again, blindfolded him, and brought him back to our lines. By no other means could the faithful beast be persuaded to leave its dead master."

Not only did animals undertake vital tasks at the Front, they also boosted morale, and the "Friend" ensured that the invaluable work and sacrifices of the animals and birds of the Great War would not be forgotten.

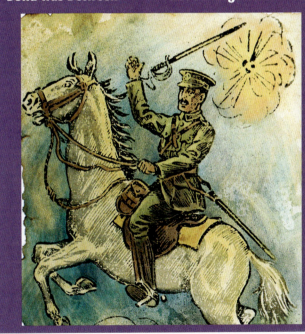

Feb 1918

The Representation of the People Act was passed in the UK, for the first time giving women over the age of thirty the right to vote.

March 1918

Following the Russian Revolution of 1917, Moscow became the capital of Soviet Russia.

July 1918

RMS Carpathia, famous for rescuing survivors of the doomed *Titanic*, was itself torpedoed and sunk by a German U-boat off the east coast of Ireland. Of the 223 people on board, 218 were rescued.

Nov 1918

Germany signed an armistice agreement with the Allies, bringing the war to an end on the 11th hour of the 11th day of the 11th month. During the four-year conflict, over 16 million people lost their lives.

On The Cover

The Great War changed the lives of those left behind, as well as those in the trenches, and the "Friend" was witness for all . . .

No. 2350. Jan. 11, 1915.

PEOPLE'S FRIEND.

THE FRIEND — FOR — EVERY HOME

HOW MEN ARE PREPARED FOR THE FIGHTING LINE.

ENCAMPED IN FRANCE.

By CAPTAIN HORACE WYNDHAM, British Expeditionary Force.

Colonel and Corporal smoke Cigarettes together.

A single bucketful of water has to do among a dozen.

(Continuation on page 26.)

Maude Crawford's fine new story, "The Price of Love," begins next week.

Jan 11, 1915

A new year had begun, but with so many of her young men fighting overseas in this "war to end all wars", Great Britain had little to celebrate.

Throughout this period the "Friend" gave faithful accounts for those left behind, and urged them to do all they could to assist the fight against the foe.

Nov 13, 1916
Animals and birds were commended for their valour.

July 24, 1916
Annie S. Swan visited a home for maimed servicemen.

May 1, 1916
Thrilling stories of devoted Red Cross nurses.

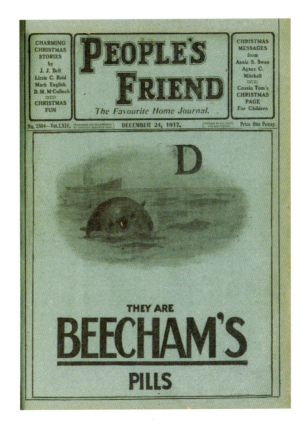

Dec 24, 1917
This witty advertisement had a sombre side.

Back Row, 3rd from left: Joe Lee; 4th from left: John B. Nicholson. Front Row, 3rd from left: Linton Andrews.

Writers At War

As war raged across Europe, the men and women whose words filled the pages of the "Friend" found themselves with new roles to play.

Joseph Lee.

SHORTLY after the outbreak of war, a group of journalists from Dundee who all worked for the publishing house of John Leng & Co. signed up to join the Black Watch. There were nine of them in total, including Joseph Lee, editor of "The People's Journal", W. Linton Andrews, editor of "The Dundee Advertiser" and John (Jack or Nick) Beveridge Nicholson, a staff writer on the "Friend", and collectively they became known as Dundee's Fighter-Writers.

In his autobiography, W. Linton Andrews wrote of the comfort and sense of solidarity he and his friends drew from each other: "Presently, to my immense joy, some of my office colleagues joined. We kept together as much as we could and called ourselves 'the Fighter-Writers' . . ."

In their first days with the battalion, they found they were better dressed and more professional than some of their fellow recruits, and so felt out of place, but once in uniform, a sense of classlessness and camaraderie developed amongst the men. Linton Andrews said later that

Linton Andrews and Jack Nicholson regularly sent back reports from the Front to Dundee's newspapers.

Joseph Lee was "the best-loved man in the Battalion".

At no point did they forget their craft; Linton Andrews and Jack Nicholson regularly sent back reports from the Front to Dundee's newspapers, while Joseph Lee contributed poetry.

In one powerful report, "Night Noises In the Trenches", Jack Nicholson vividly described the horrible truth of life at the sharp end of the conflict:

"'Hell let loose' is a description I have often seen applied to it, but in reality is not half strong enough. If any human being could properly describe a modern battle, Dante's picture of the Inferno would look like a picture of peace in contrast."

The three colleagues were brave men who stuck together; in one incident, they saved two injured men from the battlefield whilst under an onslaught of enemy fire.

Tragically, Jack Nicholson was killed by a German sniper on July 13, 1915, at the age of just twenty-one. Shot in the chest, he died almost immediately, in the arms of his friends Joseph Lee and Linton Andrews.

His death was announced with great sadness in the pages of "The People's Friend", where the Editor mourned the fact that "his bright presence will cheer us no more". Joseph Lee wrote a poem entitled "Marching" in tribute to his

Challenging Times

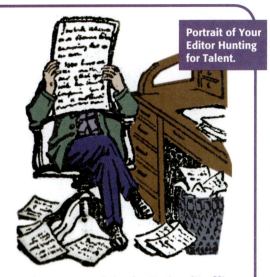

Portrait of Your Editor Hunting for Talent.

The Editor and staff of the "Friend" firmly believed it had an important role to play as hostilities raged, and that was to keep up morale at home and abroad through publishing quality stories and features. But it wasn't long before wartime shortages began to take their toll, and in 1916 the Editor advised readers to order their magazine regularly from their newsagent, else "they may find it impossible to get a copy of the paper. The number printed must be reduced."

Sourcing enough material to fill those pages presented a challenge, and initiatives such as holding a writing competition to encourage new authors, and an appeal for "girl readers" to work in the "Friend" offices and fill the gaps left by staff members involved in war work and active service, began to appear.

John Buchan described Lee's "The Green Grass" as "one of the best war poems in any language".

After the war, Lee faded into the background, and his poetry has since largely disappeared from public consciousness, though in recent years a campaign has begun to earn much-deserved recognition for Scotland's forgotten war poet.

Whilst fighting on the

Y.M.C.A. I knew that she would acquire a vast quantity of excellent material for her pen."

In 1915, Annie had a narrow escape when her home in Glasgow was destroyed during a Zeppelin raid. Undeterred, she redoubled her efforts, spending time at the Front in 1916, where she gained "a deep insight into the soldier's heart" which inspired the story of a

female literary great to be moved by the plight of the hundreds of thousands of Belgian refugees.

It has been claimed that the inspiration behind the much-loved crime fiction character Hercule Poirot dates back to this time.

It is said that a policeman called Jacques Hornais met Agatha Christie after fleeing his native Belgium in 1914, just like the fictional character.

Jacques Hornais and the author are reputed to have met after she played the piano for him in her home town of Torquay. Agatha Christie later introduced the legendary sleuth in her 1920 novel, "The Mysterious Affair At Styles". ■

Annie had a narrow escape when her home in Glasgow was destroyed during a Zeppelin raid

Annie S. Swan

young friend:

Linton on my left hand –
But, alas! poor Jack!
Marching, marching,
Quietly does he lie,
Marching, marching,
Who so sad as I?

Joseph Lee, who contributed poetry to the "Friend", published his first anthology in 1916 and met with great critical acclaim.

He was ranked alongside Rupert Brooke, Wilfred Owen and Siegfried Sassoon in terms of literary achievement, and author

front line was for men only, women writers of the time were determined to make their own mark on the war effort – and none more so than the prolific author Annie S. Swan, arguably the most popular contributor the "Friend" has ever known.

She used all of the experiences she gleaned to inform and shape her writing. In May 1916, the Editor noted: "When Annie S. Swan went to the Front as a worker under the

young English soldier, Private Bert Simmons.

She worked tirelessly to raise morale, especially amongst women, and travelled not only to the Front to encourage and enthuse the troops, but also to the USA to educate American women about the war and its effects on Britain. In 1918, for her work on behalf of Belgian refugees, Annie was given a special decoration by the King of the Belgians.

She wasn't the only

News From The Front

The "Friend" saw it as its duty to keep readers up to date with the latest developments from war zones across the world.

Details of life in the trenches were eagerly awaited by loved ones at home.

AS the conflict gained momentum, the "Friend" sought to soothe in some small way the anxieties of readers worried about loved ones by performing a new service – keeping them informed of the latest news from the Front.

"The mothers and wives of our soldiers at the Front have many anxious thoughts as to how their dear ones are faring," we reasoned, and for the duration of the war the magazine did its best to bring families torn apart by conflict a little closer by painting a picture of life at the Front and in the battlefields around the world.

No doubt being aware of the facts, dreadful as they could be, was preferable for those left behind to allowing their imaginations to run riot about what their nearest and dearest were enduring.

In a Britain beset by food shortages, it must have been a small comfort to know that the soldiers were being well fed, with one ration of food per day consisting of equal parts of meat and potatoes washed down with tea or coffee. The Tommies would occasionally enjoy the added luxury of vegetables and milk.

Keeping yourself comfortably and adequately clothed was another matter. Officers were responsible for the purchase of all their necessities which, Archibold Douglas wrote in the "Friend", was "a most absorbing and expensive affair", with a revolver costing £4, and a chest protector priced at a guinea (desirable "if he is particularly anxious to get home alive").

The magazine's own man at the Front, Private J. Beveridge Nicholson, who tragically lost his life to a German sniper in 1915, sent back reports about his experiences, including the powerful "Night Noises In The Trenches". In this article, not even the usual cheerful optimism of the "Friend" could disguise the horrible truth of war.

A keen sense of hearing, Private Nicholson told the reader, could make the difference between survival and death.

"The German bullet 'cracks' like a circus rider's whip; ours sounds more like the bursting of a soft paper bag.

"Like their rifle shots, the Germans' machine-gun reports are less muffled than ours, like the infinitely swift rapping of a door knocker. Ours might be likened to a carpet being beaten by very dexterous and intensely energetic spring cleaners armed with canes."

Keeping its readers

warfare, and it was noted that cricket players were in high demand as an accurate bowler could despatch one quickly and easily to its intended target.

Of the many technical innovations the "Friend" reported on, the one that struck most fear into the hearts of its readers was the "terrible tank".

The magazine told the story of how one of these "motor landships" ran out of fuel on the battlefield and the Germans "went after it with the avidity of prehistoric man striking a wounded mammoth".

Of course, just as today, where there is conflict there are war correspondents, people

The Allies

The appetite for information about the troops belonging to Britain's Allies was keen. In an article about the Alpini, the "picturesque" soldiers of the Italian army, readers were transported to the dangerous battles of the Dolomites and Alps, where these soldiers, specially trained in mountain warfare, engaged in precipitous battles on the high peaks.

Meanwhile, the ANZAC (Australian and New Zealand Army Corps) received the full gratitude of the "Friend" for their role in the battle at Gallipoli, at which they fought with "ready, splendid, irresistible and glorious recklessness".

An Alpini soldier of the Italian army.

The "Friend" reported that "It is no exaggeration to say that almost every man who came through that dread experience merited a decoration for bravery."

Not even the usual cheerful optimism of the "Friend" could disguise the horrible truth of war

informed about the various roles within the armed forces became a regular part of the magazine during the war years.

In 1916, an article on the "heroic chaplains" of the war paid tribute to "soldiers of the Cross who have yielded up their lives", including Father Billy O'Flynn, the "little chaplain" who was involved in the landings on the Dardanelles peninsula and who was killed whilst bringing comfort to his dying charges.

The mechanics of war was another topic that attracted the interest of readers.

"Strange Weapons Of War" described the miles of barbed wire being used in warfare, and the new and horrifying practice of electrifying it to prevent soldiers cutting it with tools.

The bomb, too, played a major part in trench

documenting the war, riding in tanks and jumping from crater to crater, photographing events like the Battle of the Somme and often coming under fire themselves, with their cameras regularly mistaken for machine guns.

The "Friend" could not have brought its readers so many reports from the fighting without their bravery and determination to share the truth.

One "Official Kinematographer" revealed that an officer had told him "I'd rather be in my shoes than yours, any day".

The Tommies were glad to see them, though. Just as reporting on the war brought solace to the folks at home, so did knowing their families had some idea of what they were going through give comfort to the troops.

"Good old movies. It's about time the people at home saw what we have to

go through," one soldier told the Kinematographer for the "Friend".

Once the conflict was over, the "Friend" continued to publish informative articles to help its readers keep up to date with the latest news.

Newspaper censorship was lifted, allowing many "thrilling stories" to be told. But, the readers were reminded, there "will be many discharged and wounded soldiers, many maimed and crippled men,

many suffering the effects of gas and shell shock.

"Let us be very kind to them, remembering that they endured all their sufferings for us. Our heroes should never know a day's want so long as they live."

It would, the Editor warned, take time for life to return to normal.

"Though the War is over, there is still a battle to be fought; let us bear our part in it with courage and effect." ■

Letters from home played a vital part in keeping up morale.

Women's Work

The ways in which women helped the war effort were many and varied.

THERE was a clear expectation that every woman left behind at home would do her bit to aid the war effort. For some, that meant going out to work and taking on jobs that had once been solely the preserve of men, such as working as a conductor on trams (though war or not, women still weren't allowed to drive them) or as a clerk in a bank.

Others took up new roles that hadn't existed before the war, becoming munitions workers or serving in the new female-only arms of the services that were swiftly created.

And then, of course, there were the many thousands of nurses who devoted themselves to tending the sick and wounded: "As for the army of nurses at home and abroad, no words are adequate to describe their heroic and self-denying labours. In this one department alone, women have done the most magnificent war service."

The quest for moss

The "Friend" was not slow to encourage its readers to seek out new ways to assist the war effort. When it became clear that shortages were risking the supply of wound dressings, a novel campaign was launched.

Readers were urged to head out into the countryside to gather sphagnum moss, which could be used as an absorbent dressing: "Now, which of you will undertake the quest for sphagnum moss? I appeal specially to lady readers, who have perhaps a little more spare time than men in these days. Thanks to the long evenings we all enjoy, there is more time for walking in daylight, and anyone living near a moor will have a capital opportunity of gathering the moss."

A job well done

Turning fresh green moss into a hygienic dressing was a labour intensive and lengthy process. One lady who worked as a moss cleaner wrote to the "Friend" to explain that this work was her way of contributing to the war effort: "At a Club near where I live I get a bagful of raw moss, which I clean in my spare time and then return. This is sent to Edinburgh Infirmary after it is dried, and is used for war dressings."

Eventually, "Friend" readers collected so much moss that the Honorary Secretary of the Red Cross Society wrote personally to thank them. Once again, these resourceful women

had risen to the challenge their Editor had set them.

Haven of refuge

And there was another challenge to come in 1916, with a campaign spearheaded by author Annie S. Swan to fund and build a YMCA hut at the Front to provide assistance and comfort to the soldiers. She had spent time in the huts in France, talking to the men, and it had moved her deeply.

The amount needed was £450, and donations soon began to pour in, along with readers' stories of what they had done to raise the money. Whip-

rounds, school concerts, craft and knitting sales; they all added up. As 1917 began, the fund totalled £1200, and the first hut was built in France, near the firing line on the Somme. A second and third followed, providing "a very haven of refuge to our men going to and coming from the trenches." Naturally, they were also well stocked with back issues of the "Friend"! ∎

The YMCA was, Annie S. Swan declared, "the soldier's home while on foreign soil."

Gifts From Home

Not long after the outbreak of war, the "Friend" was mobilising its readers to use their skills and ingenuity to ease the discomfort suffered by the troops at the Front. Behind every soldier in the battlefield was an army of women knitting and stitching to keep Tommy warm and comfortable. "Let 'ever doing' be our watchword," the magazine exhorted, "and your men will bless us."

With winter just around the corner, donations of knitted mufflers, helmets and socks were especially welcome, and they arrived by the sackload, sometimes with tobacco, cigarettes or a bar of soap, too. The "Friend" even offered a service whereby readers could send extra packages of tobacco and cigarettes for the princely sum of just sixpence.

With a staple diet of meat,

bread, chocolate and tea, mealtimes could be dull affairs for the troops, which was why the "Friend" launched its plum pudding campaign ahead of Christmas 1914: "For a shilling you can send a splendid Plum Pudding to a Soldier at the Front. Who would like to send a few?" the "Friend" asked. In total, over 3,500 were sent!

The Editor never took the sacrifices and hard work of his readers during the war years for granted, and in return, no matter how big the request, or how great the need, they invariably exceeded all expectations. Readers knitted, sewed, donated, collected and sent subscriptions in astonishing numbers: "Now that it is all over, we may congratulate ourselves on a piece of splendid patriotic work admirably and successfully accomplished. The Editor returns heartfelt thanks to all who have assisted in making the 'Friend' contributions so very handsome."

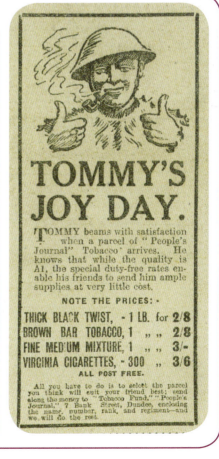

Between The Wars

For now, at least, the fighting was over, life could return to normal – and the "Friend" and its readers could look forward to the future.

Pushing The Boundaries

From attempts to climb Mount Everest to exhibitions showing off the prowess of the British Empire, things were changing . . . and fast.

PLANES, trains and automobiles all ensured that connecting city to city and further afield had never been easier.

Things were changing fast as advancements in technology ensured boundaries were constantly being pushed.

The "Friend" Editor wrote: "We are just beginning to realise the aftermath of war in the shape of many new inventions. The needs of the war set many sharp brains to work, with results that will bring untold benefits to mankind.

The Editor told of petrol-driven buses travelling to remote parts of the country

"For one thing, these two great wonder-workers – electricity and petrol – are coming to our aid in undreamt-of ways."

There was optimism that all these new advancements would now be used for good. The Editor told of petrol-driven buses travelling to remote parts of the country, while airships, aeroplanes and hydroplanes would carry letters and parcels and "convey us all on all sorts of journeys".

The Editor added, "Among its many triumphs, aviation will have nothing more striking to record than the successful crossing of the Atlantic."

Aviation rapidly "took off" and records were being set and broken. Not least of all by Amelia Earhart, who was the first female to fly solo across the Atlantic.

Explorers also set their sights high, with attempts to scale Mount Everest being documented in the pages of the "Friend".

A British team, which included George Mallory, was the first to attempt to scale it in 1921.

The "Friend" commented,

You Can't Afford To Miss It!

"The People's Friend Summer Number" was advertised (just 2d in 1922), offering more value for money for readers. Not only that, it featured amusing competitions, including one called "Seek-it-out" which had a first prize of £100, second prize of £25 and a clutch of runners-up prizes which included sewing-machines, carpet sweepers and wringers.

The "Friend" readers were reaching far-flung corners of the globe, and "The People's Friend" subscription rates meant the magazine could be sent to "any part of the world direct from the publishers for 6 months for 6s 6d; for 12 months, 13s."

1926-1931

Jan 1926

Scottish inventor John Logie Baird successfully demonstrated the first use of television.

April 1926

On April 21, Britain's longest-reigning monarch, Queen Elizabeth II, was born in Mayfair, London. The first-born child of the Duke and Duchess of York – the future King George VI and Queen Elizabeth – Princess Elizabeth became first in line to the throne upon her uncle's abdication and subsequent coronation of her parents. Elizabeth herself ascended the throne in 1952.

Aug 1927

Natural history writer Henry Williamson's much-loved and influential novel "Tarka The Otter" was published.

July 1928

The Equal Franchise Act came into effect, entitling women to equal voting rights with men.

"Until the expedition of 1921 approached its snow-clad slopes, no European had ever been within forty miles of the great mountain."

Another attempt was made the following year, and again in 1924 – when Mallory and Andrew Irvine never returned.

Of course, we now know it was to take a few more decades before Everest was conquered.

In the same year as that fateful 1924 attempt, an exhibition was held in Wembley to show off the prowess of the British Empire.

The "Friend" commented on previous exhibitions, such as the Crystal Palace Exhibition of 1851, but proclaimed that this exhibition would be the "greatest of them all".

The "Friend" pages declared, "It will illustrate practically everything connected with the British Empire. Every Colony and Dependency, with its products and its natural life, will be represented and illustrated.

"Natives – white, black, brown, yellow and red – will be seen there, living in their native houses just as they do in their own countries."

It was done on a massive scale – a complete Chinese street was created to display silks and ivory goods from Hong Kong, while thatched huts helped represent life in West Africa.

There was also the promise of "a bevy of beautiful girls who illustrate varied types of female loveliness".

Advances in

The "Crying Need Of The Moment"

Things were tough for many families throughout the Twenties and Thirties, with jobs and housing in short supply.

The "Friend" talked about the "crying need of the moment", highlighting how difficult it was for people, especially young couples, to find a home.

One newly married couple had "tramped through all the suburbs and spent money on taxis and tram fares" only for the house agents simply to shake their heads.

Thousands more found themselves in the same boat, the shortage caused because the Government had prohibited the building of new houses as men, materials, and money had all been needed for the war.

The "Friend" also told of it being quite a common thing to see advertisements offering a reward of £5 to anybody who could get the advertiser a house.

Jobs of the era included anything from a jute weaver through to a rag and bone man, and the "Friend" described the latter as being as "ragged as his wares."

One letter-writer, a jute weaver, described her day as beginning at 7.45 a.m., and finishing at 5.30 p.m., with a mile and a half to travel each way. The war was in the past, but for many, the hardship continued.

communications also ensured that people heard about the event over their own wireless sets in sitting-rooms throughout the Empire, and the address given by King George V is thought to have reached over 10 million listeners.

And when King George V and Queen Mary opened the event on St George's Day, it subsequently proved to be a resounding success, with the exhibition attracting around 17 million visitors.

Who could have guessed that not much more than a decade later, the monarchy was to be thrown into complete disarray?

Following the death of King George V in January 1936, "whose death we have not ceased to mourn", the "Friend" devoted a whole page to the new monarch, Edward VIII, which carried the headline "Our Bachelor King".

It was to become the shortest reign of any British monarch. Edward VIII soon chose to give up the throne in order to marry the twice-divorced American, Mrs Wallis Simpson.

The duty of King fell to Edward's brother, George VI.

If his father before him had found it difficult to come to terms with broadcasting, it was to be far more painful for King George VI, who suffered from a severe stammer.

The new King must have had to steel himself for his radio address to the nation in September 1939, announcing that Britain was again at war.

June 1929
On June 3, film stars Douglas Fairbanks Jr. and Joan Crawford were married.

Oct 1929
The New York Stock Exchange crashed, and "Black Tuesday" signalled the beginning of America's Great Depression.

Feb 1930
The dwarf planet Pluto, named after the Roman god of the underworld, was discovered. Though Pluto was initially classified as the furthest of the nine planets from the sun, it wasn't till 2006 that it was reclassified as a dwarf planet. It took NASA's New Horizons spacecraft almost 10 years to travel to Pluto and its five orbiting moons.

Feb 1931
On February 8, film actor and cultural icon James Dean was born in Marion, Indiana.

There was no reason for women not to have the freedom that men had long enjoyed.

The Great Outdoors

The "Friend" encouraged its readers to make the most of their leisure time by getting out into the countryside.

WRITERS at the "Friend" had always been staunch advocates of a bit of time outside. Poems celebrating the joy of being outdoors and country life had appeared since the turn of the century, as urban life grew increasingly pressured and more people flocked to the countryside for a change of pace.

The prosperity of the early 1920s was flagging by the end of the decade, but the great camping and hiking boom was an affordable way for everyone to holiday.

International travel was still beyond the reach of most, but a trip to the country was to return to simpler things. Throughout this age, the magazine returned time and time again to the subject of wandering the highways and byways.

"I seek no house when the sun sets red, I carry my lodging; its weight is light. A wisp of canvas over my head, moss for a pillow and turf for a bed, supply my needs at night."

But while early odes to the great outdoors were made mainly by male writers, it was no time at all before the "Friend" was encouraging women to get out there, too.

"Not so very long ago people would have been horrified at girls attempting such a holiday. They would have been regarded as mad, and probably refused admission to camp."

Times had changed, though. The Girl Guides had been set up in 1910 and were going from strength to strength, bringing an outdoor education to young women.

The World Association of Girl Guides and Girl Scouts was formed in 1928 and there was no reason for women not to have the freedom that men had long enjoyed.

"If you are young and fit, take my advice, you will have this year the best holiday of all."

Planning for the trip began with the choice of companion.

"Two is the right number, so choose a kindred spirit, with some endurance and a good sense of humour."

Away from the heaving seaside resorts, Britain was

1932-1938

May 1932
Aviator Amelia Earhart became the first woman to fly solo across the Atlantic Ocean.

Jan 1935
On January 8, the "King of Rock 'n' Roll", Elvis Presley, was born in Mississippi. The charismatic singer started his career with renowned Sun Records in Memphis, before embarking on a successful music and film career. A leading figure of 20th century popular culture, Elvis died at his home in 1977.

Jan 1936

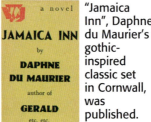

a novel

JAMAICA INN

by

DAPHNE DU MAURIER

author of

GERALD

etc. etc.

"Jamaica Inn", Daphne du Maurier's gothic-inspired classic set in Cornwall, was published.

Dec 1936
Edward VIII abdicated the throne. Succeeded by George VI, Edward married American divorcée Wallis Simpson in 1937.

just waiting to be discovered, but proper preparation was required.

What to pack, what food to take and whether to sleep under canvas or in bed and breakfasts – the "Friend" advice for those wanting to try holidays on their own under the stars was unpatronising and pragmatic.

"Don't overdress the part! There is no need to wear those dreadful hobnailed boots that usually accompany some extraordinary hiking costume."

Some mention was made of the changing times.

The country of this little island of ours is second to none

"Many girls favour shorts and are no longer looked at askance by a shocked public. It must be realised that a woman so attired needs a reasonably good figure."

And in an era of incredibly heavy canvas tents, some concessions had to be made!

"Men may manage to carry tents and enjoy a holiday at one and the same time, but women cannot."

You could get your belongings sent to your next stop on the trains, or why not try a caravan? They were still rare on the roads as it wasn't until after World War II that they took off.

"The country of this little island of ours is second to none and always seen at its best when holidaying in true gipsy style."

They had to watch out for the wildlife, though.

"Do watch you are not parked with a lot of cows. They are the most inquisitive animals going, and at times given to demolishing such things as tea towels drying on the grass, to say nothing of using your caravan as a means of alleviating itching. To be inside when a cow is butting it is most unpleasant."

Unsurprisingly, the subject of food was high up on the list of priorities. Camp food might not have been the most sophisticated cuisine, but the art of making it didn't always bring out the best in people.

"It will be found there is one of the party who believes that he or she is a heaven-born camp book, but they should be judiciously restrained."

Usually it turned out that those who boasted the least were the most capable, and food could – of course – make or break the holiday.

Ultimately, though, the "Friend" couldn't recommend the great outdoors enough.

"At the end of the week you will have forgotten all the dust and grime of city life, and remember only the beauty of the countryside and the charm of the simple life."

With the shadow of war hanging over the country, it would be a while before life would be simple again. ■

Taking To The Skies

Means of travelling the globe were coming on leaps and bounds. In 1928 the "Friend" told readers of the marvel of Croydon Airport, Britain's first significant international airport.

With three runways and a permanent presence from French and German airlines, it was cutting edge in a number of ways.

"On the air routes the twenty-four-hour system is in use."

Europe was gradually turning to this method of telling the time, with France adopting it in 1912 and Germany in 1927.

At a time before security and lengthy check-in lines, air travel was a simpler affair.

"Aeroplanes come and go with much less fuss than a railway train leaves a big terminus."

It sounds like a far cry from modern airports!

Air travel was on a different scale in those early days. Then, about 40 planes a day flew from Croydon, compared to over 650 a day at Heathrow 90 years later.

Imperial Airways was the British national carrier, running services up until 1939. Imperial was also the first ever to show a film on a flight, screening "The Lost World" in 1925 on a London to Paris route.

Alamy.

Jan 1937
On January 8, James Bond theme tune songstress Shirley Bassey was born in Cardiff.

May 1937
The Hindenburg airship disaster occurred in New Jersey, USA, marking the end of passenger airship travel.

iStock

May 1937
The Golden Gate Bridge opened. Named after the Golden Strait, the stretch of water between San Francisco Bay and the Pacific Ocean, construction began on the bridge in 1933. With a suspension span of 1.2 miles, the "international orange"-painted Golden Gate was soon established as an American landmark in engineering.

July 1938
On July 30, DC Thomson's "The Beano", the longest-running weekly comic, was first published.

On The Cover

The end of the Roaring Twenties marked the magazine's Diamond Jubilee. The "Friend" was now sixty years old!

Dec 15, 1923

The "Friend" had witnessed many changes since its inception – the reigns of three British sovereigns; revolutions and wars; the rise and fall of thrones and kingdoms. But there was still a desire to supply "the bright and friendly spirit that ought to animate a paper bearing the title of the 'People's Friend'."

Dec 21, 1929

The "Friend" was now "The Household Favourite".

Jan 20, 1934

"A romance of the Old Country and Great Dominion".

July 7, 1934

Set on a cruise ship, this story was one of a series.

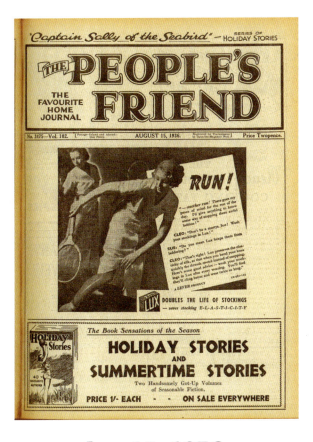

Aug 15, 1936

An age when tennis was played in stockings!

Annie S. Swan

Annie, Our Storyteller

Over a staggering sixty-three years, this well-loved writer stayed constant to the "Friend" and shared its journey . . .

IN this anniversary year we cannot forget the writer who enjoyed a special relationship with the "Friend" for very many years. Annie S. Swan was dearly loved by readers, who were great fans of her serials and short stories, all full of charm and homely appeal. She also wrote over 150 novels.

The stories she told were simple, home-spun and unashamedly romantic. She knew her audience and told the tales exactly as they wished to hear them.

But her own life story was just as fascinating.

She was born in 1859 in Berwickshire. After an education at Ladies College, Edinburgh, she married a Fife schoolteacher, James Burnett-Smith, who was studying to be a doctor. During this time, in 1881, Annie wrote her first story for the "Friend" at the age of twenty-one.

The couple moved to Edinburgh, a brave decision which meant it was only Annie's storywriting keeping the pair afloat.

After James qualified they moved to London, where he built up a successful practice in Camden Square.

The couple had two children — Edward and Effie. Tragically, Edward died as a schoolboy in a shooting accident, something his devoted father always blamed himself for, since he was the one who had gifted the rifle to Edward.

The family bravely carried on. Effie grew to be the chief mainstay and comforter of her mother's life in later years. During World War I both ladies visited the battlefields of France to talk to the troops, Effie staying behind to assist in war work.

Seeking a rest from their hectic London life, the family moved to Hertford, the doctor setting up practice there prior to joining up in the Black Watch as the war progressed.

During this time the family home was bombed in a Zeppelin raid, an event which obviously shook Annie.

"I find it difficult to describe that appalling five minutes' interlude, while the monster ship with its death-dealing cargo passed slowly over our town, visiting us last and dropping eight bombs on our house and garden."

An invitation came to go to America on a mission for food, shortages having become so desperate that the situation was serious. Her husband and daughter were on active service so Annie accepted, and toured the United States, giving talks and appealing for aid.

She was assisted in this by Herbert Hoover, and met many notables including Theodore Roosevelt, Howard Heinz, the Kelloggs and Rockefellers.

"It would not be easy to over-estimate the good she did," the British Ministry of Information reported.

Though it was suggested she be awarded the CBE, it never materialised, though she did receive one in 1930 for "literary and public services".

After the war, Annie took up an interest in politics, and in 1922 stood as a Liberal candidate in Glasgow. She was unsuccessful, but the experience had its lighter side. One canvasser approached two ladies living adjacent to each other on a landing, both with different political views: "Weel, if you're no' gaun to vote for Annie Swan, ye can buy yer ain 'People's Friend' after this!"

Dr Burnett-Smith's health began to fail, and they decided to return to Scotland. They settled in Bandrum, near Dunfermline, where they

PRICE 2/-

remained till his death in 1927.

Those were happy days, during which Annie opened countless bazaars and supported good causes, including the "Friend"'s own "Love Darg".

And she went on writing until her death in 1943 at Gullane, outside Edinburgh. ■

Annie and her daughter Effie at Gullane.

Royal Connections

Dr James Burnett-Smith, her husband.

During their time in London the Burnett-Smiths mixed with the literary giants of the day: Thomas Hardy, Sir James Barrie and Sir Arthur Conan Doyle.

Barrie said he wished he had Annie S. Swan's storytelling gift, and Annie's presentation before Queen Victoria came about after the Dowager Duchess of Atholl had read one of her Perthshire-based stories. The Queen later invited her to Court, an honour which Annie recalled with mixed emotions.

"Only the very strong could enjoy the rigours of a March Court at Buckingham Palace in those days. First, the long wait in the Mall; in those days there was no Thermos providing comforting hot drinks, and no refreshments of any kind, not even a cup of tea in the palace.

"Certainly there was a fire in the large dressing-room, but the toilet arrangements were ghastly – in fact they were non-existent. We were always thankful when it was a small attendance, so that we could get quickly away. But four hours was the usual length of the ordeal."

To the last Annie retained what she described as "my long and happy connection" with the "Friend".

"The hold of that unpretentious magazine on the public, not only in Scotland, but wherever Scots folk are to be found, is one of the romances of the newspaper world. It has no rival, though many have tried to enter the lists against it. Its public has been loyal and faithful to me for over fifty years, and there is no sign of waning enthusiasm even yet.

"'The People's Friend' has always been ably edited by men who knew their public, its limitations, and its quality."

In return, the magazine's eulogy to her in July 1943 described her passing as a personal loss: "Her memory will long be cherished and kept green in the homes and hearts of thousands who were the gainers by her gracious influence upon them."

The Great Giveaway

From needle-threaders to plastic aprons, "The People's Friend" has long delighted in giving readers more than fantastic fiction!

OVER the past 150 years the "Friend" has given away an astonishing variety of gifts bearing its name.

Twenty-five years ago there was still on the go a "Friend" carpet sweeper from 1913, while in 1904 you could check the weather forecast with the "Friend" barometer. One lucky competition winner in the 1890s took possession of a grand piano!

A favourite item, a jelly pan, was given as a joint prize in 1920 between the "Friend" and its sister paper, "My Weekly". It was returned years later by its kind owner, who felt it was time it "came home", and it now accompanies staff whenever they go out to give talks on the magazine.

No doubt many households in Britain still have whisks, spatulas and conversion charts in kitchen drawers. Do write in and say, won't you? ■

Are You in Want of a New Jelly Pan?

Try Our Jam and Jelly-Making Competition.

The Jam-making season is fast approaching, and the above competition is sure to interest all " Friend" Housewives, who must have by them numerous recipes for making both Jam and Jelly, also various hints on Jam-making.

1. FOR THE BEST RECIPE FOR MAKING JAM.
   First Prize—Splendid Aluminium Jelly Pan, with Consolation Gifts of Brass Jelly Pans.
2. FOR THE BEST RECIPE FOR MAKING JELLY.
   First Prize—Splendid Aluminium Jelly Pan, with Consolation Gifts of Brass Jelly Pans.
3. FOR THE BEST HINT ON JAM AND JELLY-MAKING.
   First Prize—Splendid Aluminium Jelly Pan, with Consolation gifts of Brass Jelly Pans.

1920
The above competition gave away aluminium jelly pans as well as brass ones.

AN EXCITING GIFT FOR YOU!

FREE

THE "PEOPLE'S FRIEND" HOUSEHOLD APRON

* Full Length—Perfect For Every Job Around The House
* Waterproof
* Attractively Finished With A Flower Motif

1972
This one-size-fits-all apron would certainly have been useful, if perhaps not exactly exciting as stated!

FREE!

Presented With THE PEOPLE'S FRIEND

Your Good Health Diary 1979

Just The Right Size For Slipping Into Your Handbag

All The Features You Look For In A Useful Diary

Many Pages Packed With Tips — First Aid In The Home — A Mother's Guide To Children's Illnesses

And Lots More Hints And Advice

LOOK OUT FOR IT IN

NEXT WEEK'S "FRIEND"

1979
This diary was full of first-aid advice for out and about or in the home, and also had a guide to children's illnesses.

A Dainty New Year Gift

My Lady's Coronation Calendar

A Lovely Calendar for 1937
With Exquisite Picture

A Beautiful and Useful Present

GIVEN FREE

The Coronation Calendar, prepared some time ago, is presented as a souvenir of recent striking events.

Inside Every Copy of the
'PEOPLE'S FRIEND' NEXT WEEK

1937

This coronation calendar from 1937 was overtaken by events, as King Edward VIII announced his abdication on December 10, 1936.

1927

These "Friendship cards", bearing inspiring verses, were designed to be hung on the wall.

1905

"Friend" biscuits were offered as a prize on the Letters page and showed the masthead.

When day is done and twilight falls
On homestead, street, or lonely wood,
'Tis gladsome when the mind recalls
No chances missed of doing good.

Copyright

Although to-day your skies seem grey,
To-morrow they'll be blue,
Remember, when your luck seems out,
It's bound to turn without a doubt
And dearest hopes come true.
Just do your bit and show your grit,
Refrain from vain repining.
When worries all around you loom
Remember, somewhere through the gloom,
God's star of hope is shining.

THE PEOPLE'S FRIEND

A Fisher Girl

I don't think I have seen a letter from a fisher girl on your page. Our work is very interesting, as in the summer time we have to go along with the fishermen to work at the herrings, which lasts for a period from two and a half to three months, and then in autumn we go to Yarmouth, which is a fine change for us. When we come home we have to mend the herring nets; our hours are from eight in the morning till eight at night. We are always looking forward to Friday for our "Friend", which we enjoy reading very much, and I am sure we would enjoy a cup of your tea when we come home at night.

Home From Home

Among the letters to your dear self I have never seen one from a wee country mouse now lost in a big city. I am engaged as stenographer in a large engineering firm in the second city of the British Isles, but my home is in the far north. If it were not that I have been lucky finding a real home in a hospice – a boarding-house for girls – where there are about 30 girls from all parts of Scotland and Ireland, I would feel very often homesick.

The dear old "Friend" finds a cosy corner with us, and it would give you great pleasure to see so many heads poring over the latest innovation – cross-word puzzles.

Hielan' Lassie

I belong to the Hebrides. In order to obtain a livelihood I had to leave the islands and seek work in Glasgow. I visit my island home once a year and always look forward to my rest on the lonely spot not far from St Kilda. We are supposed to be fifty years behind the times so, Uncle Jack, you should pay us a visit and see all our strange customs. The island is now doing better in the way of industry, giving the men work, also the young girls and women. If you have ever heard of Harris tweeds you will know the place I speak of. Harris.

Letters From Far And Near

In 1924 a constant stream of letters poured on to the desk of "Uncle Jack", as readers described their daily lives. From Hebridean isles to bustling cities, they had one thing in common – the hope of winning a coveted "Friend" tea caddy.

A Land Girl

I have never come across a letter from a land-girl niece. I have worked on the land for a good while now. It is a healthy job, but cold in winter. I begin in winter when daylight comes in, and finish when it begins to get dark. Of course, we begin earlier in the summer, for it is early daylight then. Just now we are busy pulling turnips to get them stored to last the cattle all winter. Our next job will be to spread manure to let the men get on with the ploughing.

From The Outer Hebrides

I wonder if this will be your first letter from the Outer Hebrides? The other day a friend and I realised from where we were standing we could see the outline of St Kilda. It made us realise our own good fortune.

The distress in the Highlands is very evident in some parts of this island. The wet summer made it impossible for the people to get home their annual supply of peats, and now during the severe winter we are having it can readily be understood how the majority of them must be suffering. Small wonder that Hebrideans are emigrating in their thousands.

A Lady "Commercial"

I think I'm about the youngest lady traveller. I am 22. At first I found things very trying, but having been blessed with good nature, patience and a "gift of the gab" I have managed wonderfully and am winning through. I have a town route meantime, and most shops sell papers, so if I don't get my "Friend" at the first call I make sure of it at the last.

Flapper

I am one of the little wheels in the great business machine of the world; indeed, I am only a little flapper engaged as a typist in a city office. The office is dusty and dingy, but we are a very cheerful company who work there. We all look forward to Thursday, for that is the day when we are introduced to a new "Friend". I'm afraid there is a lot of time spent listening for the boss while we all have a surreptitious peep to see how our heroines' romances are progressing.

The Budding Teacher

I am about to be one of those much-criticised individuals, namely, a teacher. I am at college, and hope to be a full-fledged teacher soon. As it is, all the students have one day a week out teaching in the city schools. I go to a poor district, and I never had thought there could be such poverty and misery till I had proof of it. I stay in one of the hostels in connection with college. There are 60 girls in it, so you will have an idea of the row there is at mealtimes. Our troubles begin at seven in the morning when the rising bell goes. We are kept going until "lights out" goes at 10.30 p.m. We have great times in our rooms and midnight feasts are not unknown.

Photography For Girls

You have had letters from nieces in all professions, I think, unless that of photography, the most interesting career a girl can take up. It is wonderful what strides photography has made within the last few years. What with fast plates, fast lenses, electric light installations &c., we are independent of the weather. In times gone by a photograph could only be taken on a good day, and before darkness fell. Now that does not matter.

The general public have some queer ideas about photography. For instance, they think that all that has to be done is to "squeeze the ball". They little know that that is the easy part of it. After the plate has been exposed it has to be developed, fixed, washed, dried and retouched, and then the print is made, which in its turn has to be exposed, developed, fixed, washed, dried, mounted and finished. So you see what a tremendous amount of work is entailed from the time the sitter faces the camera.

World War II

History repeated itself with the outbreak of World War II in 1939, and once again the "Friend" would do its utmost to bring cheer and comfort to its readers.

82

Poetry Of The War

Edith Vassie's poem "Unrest" marked the first mention of war in the "Friend", and thereafter its writers produced some poignant commentary.

A.N. Ford's charming 1940 springtime poem expressed the longing of a wife for her beloved as the seasons rolled around again.

"I pray for peaceful springtimes soon, when, by some happy chance, I'll hold you close and ask you – 'Are there daffodils in France?'"

Contact with soldiers was easier than in WWI and the magazine received plenty of letters from the sharp end of the conflict.

G.B. wrote of moving on from friendships in temporary quarters. Those in the Forces were together for only a short time, which led to more goodbyes than usual.

"Must one always part with friends? Are there never journey's ends?"

To G.B. it was proof there was goodness left in all of us, and hope for all of us, because it was so sad to have to say farewell.

The Skies Darken Again

As war broke out once more, the "Friend" was determined to be a companion to its readers.

WITH several weeks between a magazine issue being completed and the copies actually appearing on the shelves, it took a while before the war was mentioned and the "Friend" caught up with events.

In the September 9 issue, poet E.A. Vassie lamented that "dark across the world the war clouds hang", but beseeched readers to look to the woods and the hills for comfort. Evidence of God's reassuring presence was there.

In September 23, the Editor wrote of the battle having begun, with the heaviness of it being all too familiar.

"One day the guns will cease their firing, and love and charity will pervade in the hearts of all men."

Until that day, the staff had high hopes of being of service during the times ahead, as a comfort and cheer, and they encouraged readers to offer the same service for each other.

Already a stoic attitude ran through their commentary: "It is the duty

Could our readers help the young mothers often evacuated with their children? Eleanor felt sure of it

of all of us to keep as cheerful as we can."

The magazine began to offer readers a chance to help with their skills.

The Love Darg appealed for garments for wounded soldiers, convertible mitt patterns appeared, and with scarcity about to hit the Home Front, too, Eleanor (the "Friend's" home economist) offered pages of advice, and Kitty, her recipes.

Could readers help the young mothers often evacuated with their children? Eleanor felt sure of it and asserted that domestic wisdom was a gift to be passed on. Why, one woman had never made a pot of soup in her life!

"As for the mysteries of a steak pudding – they left her positively breathless."

It was a real social service, Eleanor said, to pass on these skills to the next generation, and would doubtless help them no end in the future when they returned to the towns and cities.

An evacuee wrote about her new life in the country, commenting on the uncommon dark at night and how much she was

1939-1941

Aug 1939
The fantasy adventure film "The Wizard Of Oz", starring Judy Garland, was released in America.

Sept 1939
On September 1, Adolf Hitler's Nazi Germany invaded Poland, resulting in the outbreak of World War II. Shortly after, Britain and France declared war on Germany. The ensuing war between the Allied and Axis Powers was to last for six years, with an estimated 50 to 80 million fatalities.

June 1940
British Prime Minister Winston Churchill's famous speech, "We Shall Fight On The Beaches", was delivered to the House of Commons.

August 1940
"Gone With The Wind" star Vivien Leigh and stage and screen star Laurence Olivier were married.

enjoying the change of scenery.

Uncle Jack's tea caddy prize was keenly sought after, and readers would regularly end their letters by pointing out how much better life would be if they had some quality tea leaves.

Many wrote to Uncle Jack from the countryside, noting that the upheaval of the move had been greatly lessened by a chance to eat home-cooked food, breathe fresh air and explore new and pleasant rural surroundings. Some were delighted to get away from the smoky cities for a spell.

It was an interesting sign of just how diverse the readership would become during the war, when a nostalgia for home and for simpler times would drive those on the Front to find comfort in the "Friend", too.

"We, in this barrack room, appreciate . . . your paper, as it reminds us of home," one soldier wrote.

That same soldier was

sadly a veteran of the Great War, too, but was glad that in this new conflict the accommodation proved a little more civilised.

Of course, many of the readers remembered the Great War – "A Constant Reader", who was putting pen to paper to get a copy of the "War-time Knitting

Leaflet", still had her copy of the knitting leaflet from the last conflict.

"I hope we won't be working for the Forces for over four years this time," she said.

The magazine's role was to improve the morale of those on the Home Front, and much was made of the importance of a cheerful

attitude, illustrated in the October 21 issue by an observation from a "foreigner":

"I can't understand you Britishers. When you're happy, you go about as if you were bored with life; but when you're up against it, you smile as though everything in the world was just perfect." ■

Letters from loved ones kept up the spirits of those on the Front.

Sept 1940

The Jeep, a 4x4 all-terrain reconnaissance vehicle, was tested for the US Army.

April 1941

Compton Mackenzie's comic novel "The Monarch Of The Glen", featuring the fictional Glenbogle Estate, was published.

May 1941

The first jet engine aircraft took flight. It was while training as a Pilot Officer that Frank Whittle conceived the idea of jet-powered flight. As early as 1930, Whittle applied for a patent, and later, with financial backing and Air Ministry approval, the turbo-jet engine project was born.

Dec 1941

The United States Naval base at Pearl Harbor was attacked by the Japanese navy, triggering America's entry into World War II.

The Men In Command

The "Friend" aimed to provide comfort and reassurance to its readers by profiling the qualities of the Allied leadership.

As it had during World War I, the "Friend" kept its readers supplied with information about the conflict to help people feel connected to their fighting family members.

The military figures at the head of Britain's Forces were the subject of keen attention.

There was a change in tone from the magazine's Great War features, though. Perhaps this was a response to the feeling that too many of the lives lost in the Great War had been casualties of a cavalier attitude to the wellbeing of the men.

With vast numbers sent from the trenches to their

It was important to reassure readers that our new leaders had a healthy respect for the lives under their command

deaths for little tactical progress, it had been a war with no strategic precedent.

In truth, warfare had changed so much during those four years of World War I that few traditional tactics were still relevant, and the military minds of the day struggled to catch up. But it was important, the "Friend" believed, to reassure readers that our new leaders had a healthy respect for the lives under their command.

As during the first conflict, these informative features did not run for the whole length of the war but appeared sporadically in just the first few years.

Perhaps once the realities of war bit, the appetite for information dwindled and readers became more concerned with how they could help.

Picking out a few key figures, the profiles began at the top with General Gamelin, Chief of the Allied Armies.

The series devoted full pages (at a time when only stories were accorded such space) to surprisingly in-depth looks at the lives and characters of these men.

Uncle Jack's Weekend Message

Thoughts from letters page editor Uncle Jack.

Freedom is very precious.
It is worth suffering for; worth fighting for.
I heard a lark high in the sky,
Singing sic a cheery song,
That I made up my mind tae try

Tae aye be cheery a' day long.
We see you sweeping o'er the sky,
We, who owe so much to few,
Salute to all of you who fly;
May God be always guarding you.

1942-1944

Jan 1942
On January 17, heavyweight boxing champion Muhammad Ali was born in Louisville, Kentucky.

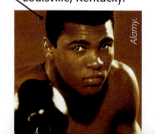

Jan 1942
The first recording of Desert Island Discs took place in the BBC's bomb-damaged Maida Vale studios. Aired on the Forces Programme, the show involved the presenter asking a well-known person to choose eight gramophone records they would take with them if they were cast away on a desert island.

Alamy.

Nov 1942
General Montgomery's 8th Army defeated Rommel's Afrika Korps in the second battle of El Alamein.

Jan 1943
The wartime romance film "Casablanca", starring Humphrey Bogart and Ingrid Bergman, premiered in London.

Alamy.

Gamelin, the "Friend" declared, "has the broad brow of a scholar and the finely-chiselled face of an artist."

The last two sentences of Gamelin's introduction revealed the real reason why readers were being told such detail about these men. It was

Gone were the days when commanders paid more attention to their men's appearance than to the training they received

important for the general public to know that their leaders cared about each and every fighting man, so that they could all rest a little easier in that knowledge.

"The women of France and Britain can be certain that Gamelin will not allow the lives of their sons, husbands and brothers to be needlessly wasted."

Things had changed in the Forces.

"Gone are the days when the British Army was commanded by men who paid more attention to the smart appearance of their men than to the training they received," an article in

The Colonials Are Coming!

Britain's fighting forces were bolstered by the contribution of men from its overseas territories. Writer Robert Wishart penned an article about them, after hearing of an encounter with a Canadian ex-soldier on a London bus.

The soldier had chastised the British people he'd met for not being quick to welcome strangers, and Wishart urged readers to do all they could to address this.

"Unless we can forget our stupid don't-speak-unless-spoken-to attitude, and give the Colonials the same open-hearted welcome they would give us in their countries, there is a big danger that all the good will may be dispelled."

To make it a little easier, Wishart told readers more about the men they might meet.

"You will find them extremely easy to get on with," he advised.

Australians tended to get nostalgic about their home climate when the cold arrived, he went on, "but to get on really well with Australians, the most important asset is a sense of humour." If you couldn't laugh at yourself, there was no doubt the Australians would do it for you!

Canadians were "self-reliant and large and genial, with a partiality for waffles and the habit of eating everything possible with a fork alone."

But, like the Australians and New Zealanders, their "most striking characteristic was that of friendliness". Our allies were good men to know.

praise of Sir John Dill began.

Sir John was "typical of the new type of British officer: quiet, well-read, cultured experts at their job."

The "fresh-complexioned, tight-lipped and somewhat sombre" Air Chief Marshall Sir Cyril Newall was the man entrusted with the defence of our skies.

When it came to describing the Chief of the Imperial General Staff, "Big Bill" Ironside, it was hard to know where to begin.

"He measures six foot four and weighs eighteen stone. He speaks sixteen languages and can express his disapproval of people or things in one or two more."

Bill went on to recognise the future Shah of Iran as a Cossack of the Russian Imperial Army, spotting something in his character that he admired.

Poland's General Sikorski was the "organising genius" behind the country's army, which it was hoped would lead a sterling resistance in a country that had time and again been caught between a rock and a hard place.

As the conflict heightened and these biographies disappeared from the magazine's pages, one of the last factual features about the war came in 1940, when the "Friend" printed an explanation of Finland's landscape ("the country of a thousand forests") as the devastating Winter War took grip. ■

Dec 1943

"Bevin Boys", eligible conscripts, were called up by ballot to work in British coal mines.

Feb 1944

Based at Bletchley Park, the first code-breaking computer, Colossus Mark 1, came into operation.

June 1944

The D-Day Landings began on the beaches of Normandy. Codenamed Operation Overlord, the Allied Forces, consisting of British, American and Canadian troops, amassed on five beaches of France's Normandy coastline. The amphibious, paratrooper and glider landings were a turning point in the war, resulting in the liberation of Western Europe.

Dec 1944

Band leader Glenn Miller tragically died when the aircraft he was travelling in disappeared over the English Channel.

Returning To The Shelves

Adverts promised the return of some of people's favourite household items.

1 Heinz's famous 57 varieties had been honed down to the bare minimum, but one by one they were to make their return. Heinz were actually producing 60 products by then, but they liked the number. Now they produce 5,700 products around the world.

2 During the war Singer Sewing Machines had ceased manufacture, but domestic production soon began again. You could visit a Singer shop and add your name to the waiting list, and a new machine would eventually be delivered.

3 Scottish firm Duncan were delighted to announce their Hazelnut Milk Chocolate was coming back. "Don't forget, the watchword is 'nuts in chocolate'."

Keep a sharp look-out on all sweet shops—Duncan Hazelnut Milk Chocolate is coming back, and don't forget the watchword is 'nuts in chocolate.'
DUNCAN *The Scots word for Chocolate*

A Time To Heal

Once again, the country had to set its mind to the business of getting back to normal.

THE ordinary person might be pardoned for feeling a little bewildered. Just how is he, or she, to function in this great programme which is to set us on our feet again?"

The Editor observed that everyone was a little lost after the intense sense of purpose that the war had given them, and made a point of stressing that women should give up their jobs and return to their domestic lives, where they were urgently needed.

"There's nothing in the factory can take the place of home," poet E.A.G penned in early 1944. With the conflict swinging heavily in favour of the Allies, people were starting to think ahead.

It was another turning point for Britain's women, who once again had found themselves more than up to the challenge of doing the work formerly carried out by men.

However, it seemed the jobs they'd filled so ably were to be taken away from them, and few would remain in full-time employment.

A letter from an Army man to Uncle Jack tried to persuade women that maintaining the Home Front was just as valuable as employment outside the home.

Writer B.L.A. had been surprised to see a letter on

At the end of the paper shortage the Editor reassured readers that they could buy their own copies again in shops

Uncle Jack's page from "A Married Woman Who Works."

"I have been in the Army for over five years now, and in all my travels I have not met a married woman who does not work! We husbands in the Forces salute with pride our wives who keep a home together in these difficult times."

The Editor was happy to weigh in on any debate arising from readers' letters. For example, when summer rolled around in 1944, school leavers were considering their options for the future.

The Editor sternly insisted that children themselves should have the final say. He must have had a few angry letters about that, as he was still defending those statements in August that year!

"Some readers disagree with much that I said, and tell me so in plain, blunt language."

Whatever the age of the pupil, though, all agreed it was important that children got out and enjoyed the summer in the great outdoors.

It was what the soldiers were fighting for, the "Friend" told readers – an outdoors to explore and the ability to do so. The happiness of the next generation was uppermost in everyone's minds.

1945-1946

Feb 1945
A young Princess Elizabeth, later to become Queen Elizabeth II, joined the Auxiliary Territorial Service.

May 1945
On May 8, VE Day was celebrated in Britain, marking the end of the war in Europe. A national holiday was declared amid colourful parades and street parties. Prime Minister Winston Churchill addressed the nation via a radio broadcast, and later he appeared along with members of the Royal Family on the balcony of Buckingham Palace to jubilant crowds.

May 1945
Golden Age of Hollywood movie stars Humphrey Bogart and Lauren Bacall were married.

Oct 1945
The microwave oven was patented after its engineer inventor, Percy Spencer, noticed his chocolate bar had been melted by nearby radar equipment.

"The world we have been fighting for during five enduring years is going to require everybody's help once the war is won."

Poems and stories looked forward to the men returning home and praised the boys for their adventures overseas, but the magazine was by no means oblivious to the loss of life.

Although the total number of casualties was the highest yet at around 60 million (3% of the world's population), under 400,000 British military staff perished as opposed to 700,000 in the Great War.

The Soviet Union and China bore the brunt of the losses.

Edith Vassie's touching poem "There Are No Dead" explained, "Not gone from us, those ones whom we have lost, But only on in front a little way," offering comfort to the many in grief.

Hope of the war ending came in 1945, with the Editor commenting that punishment for the enemy should be thorough.

Though many readers had written to the "Friend" about the need for tolerance and clemency in the settling of accounts after the war, the Editor was adamant that leniency after the last conflict had done much to cause the second.

Letters to the magazine throughout 1946 indicated more than a little sadness from those who had returned home and left behind great friends amongst the land girls and other women's services.

Miss E.M'D. from

The war was over, and it was time for the hard work of rebuilding the nation to begin.

Craigmore had left with "suitable for re-enlistment" stamped on her conduct sheet, and wondered if she'd ever get the chance.

The world was not quick to get back to normal.

Rationing still held the country in the grip of austerity, and many a soldier returned home to be surprised that privations there were almost as severe as those at the Fronts.

Whilst Kitty was still giving advice on how to make the most of life with

clothing coupons, the "Friend" bemoaned the fact that the government seemed to concern itself overly with such things as the number of pleats or buttons on new clothing when there were more pressing concerns.

It was important for the rebuilding of the nation that morale should be kept as high as possible, but the "Friend" thought the continuation of rationing, and the bureaucracy in almost every area of life, was doing little to help.

Surely good food and an end to dowdiness were the road to a brighter future?

With the end of the paper shortage, the Editor spent much of 1946 reassuring readers that they would now be able to buy their own copies of the "Friend" once again in shops. There was no longer any need to pass on copies between friends and neighbours.

Also, subscriptions could resume to overseas readers.

Plenty of reading for everyone! ■

Sept 1946
On September 2, World War II ended when Japan signed an act of unconditional surrender on board the *USS Missouri*.

Oct 1946
The high IQ society MENSA, the Latin name for table, denoting a round table where all members are equal, was formed.

Dec 1946
The aftermath of World War II saw the formation of the United Nations International Children's Emergency Fund (UNICEF), which provided humanitarian aid to children and their mothers.

Dec 1946
On December 18, Academy Award-winning film director Steven Spielberg was born in Cincinnati, Ohio.

On The Cover

Once again at war, and once again the "Friend" stood shoulder to shoulder with the nation and its Allies . . .

Auld Farrant Things' By Martin Douglas. | Complete Stories | 'Miss Joanna Meets Herself' By Mary Elder.

THE PEOPLE'S FRIEND

THE FAVOURITE HOME JOURNAL

No. 3943—Vol. 120. Founded in 1869. AUGUST 4, 1945. Registered for Transmission by Canadian Magazine Post. Price Twopence.

Keeping up the good work

In peace, as in war, Miss Naffy goes on, bringing refreshment and relaxation to the Forces. The end of the European war has not lightened her task and she still needs the help of many more girls who are willing to volunteer for service with Naafi, either at home or overseas. Full details from your local Employment Exchange.

NAAFI

THE OFFICIAL CANTEEN ORGANISATION FOR H.M. FORCES

Aug 4, 1945

Every issue reflected a world in conflict. Both businesses and the war department exhorted civilians to save fuel and keep as healthy as possible. All daily life was geared towards the war effort. Even the children's page got involved, with Will and Wag diligently collecting scrap iron. Here, thankfully, the end was in sight.

February 28, 1942

Helping the war effort by washing wisely.

January 2, 1943

Night air-raids added to poor sleep and nerves.

June 19, 1943

A plea to keep rations for those who needed them most.

Sept 15, 1945

A familiar name, relishing the taste of freedom.

Keep Calm And Carry On

Britain might have been a different place in wartime, but some things could be relied upon to remain unchanged . . .

AS Britain marched to war for the second time, the "Friend" kept a stiff upper lip and did its best to continue as normally as possible.

In fact, apart from the adverts, which almost immediately began to mention rationing, it seems to have been decided to make sure that the conflict would have as little impact as possible on the world of the "Friend".

The aim of the magazine in those uncertain years was to provide an element of constancy and normality.

Everything within its pages was the same as ever, with uplifting stories, practical household tips from Kitty and Eleanor and gardening advice from Adam, Junior.

The Editor would refer in passing to "these troubled times", but it was in Uncle Jack's Corner that the fact that the country was at war quickly became apparent.

Shrink To Fit

As time went on, life at war slowly became normality and this began to be reflected more in the pages of the "Friend". In March 1942, an Important Announcement notified readers that "Owing to the

> **IMPORTANT ANNOUNCEMENT**
>
> OWING to the extreme scarcity of paper, the "People's Friend," in common with other publications, must undergo some reductions in size. You will continue to get your copy each week, but alternate issues will be somewhat smaller than usual. Despite this essential measure, you will enjoy the same amount of reading matter, for we do not intend to reduce the number of stories in any way. To make this possible, however, Kitty, Eleanor, and Lizette may meantime find on occasions the space at their disposal a little more limited, but they will still be offering you whenever possible their fullest help and guidance.

extreme scarcity of paper, 'The People's Friend', in common with other publications, must undergo some reductions in size. You will continue to get your copy each week, but alternate issues will be somewhat smaller than usual. Despite this

essential measure, you will enjoy the same amount of reading matter, for we do not intend to reduce the amount of stories in any way.

"To make this possible, however, Kitty, Eleanor and Lizette may meantime find on occasions the space at their disposal a little more limited, but they will still be offering you whenever possible their fullest help and guidance."

The magazine dropped from 20 pages to 16, and the font size was noticibly reduced in order to squeeze more words on to each one. The adverts, too, shrank from full pages to a quarter of a page or less.

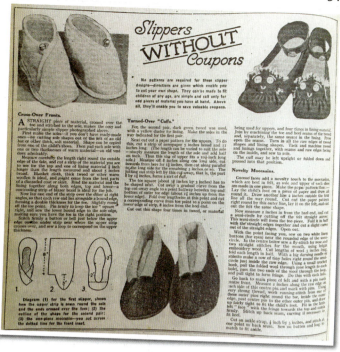

Pass It On

Reminders appeared regularly throughout the magazine to keep on saving paper. To this end, the Editor began to advocate the passing on of copies of the "Friend".

"Mrs J Armstrong, of Stornoway, tells me of the various people who read her copy. I am happy so many do. It is a kindly thing to pass your copy to someone who can't get the 'Friend' because of wartime restrictions."

It is worth mentioning, perhaps, that once the war was over the Editor made many subsequent pleas for readers to go back to buying their own copies, but sadly this is a battle we have been fighting ever since!

In addition to Kitty and Eleanor losing space, Cousin Tom's Children's Corner dropped down to half a page most weeks, but the page given to Uncle Jack, the best-known point of contact for the readers, stayed much the same.

In 1943 the Editor wrote, "Eleanor tells me that recently her postbag has contained many requests for special hints and instructions that are particularly desirable in these wartime days."

Features began to appear with titles like "Slippers Without Coupons" and "It Was Once A Scarf!"

However, the Love Darg appeals continued as usual, though its competitions were discontinued.

"We appreciate the difficulty of procuring wool and materials," readers were told, "but many active knitters will find it possible to undo jumpers and so forth that have outlived their usefulness. The need for such gifts at this time cannot be over-emphasised – it is, indeed, greater than ever."

Even in such difficult times the "Friend" readers rallied round to help those less fortunate than themselves – as they continue to do so generously today. ■

Paper Cuts

While the soldiers, sailors and airmen were doing battle with the enemy, those left at home had their own battles to fight day by day.

In addition to coping with rationing, taking on the work of the men who were in the Armed Forces – and being expected to wear a cheerful smile while doing it – the British people were exhorted by the government to recycle everything they possibly could, from food scraps to rubber bands.

Salvaged paper was recycled for newspaper or packaging products, or was sold to raise vital funds for the war campaign.

Paper was in high demand, as we have already seen.

Most newspapers and periodicals did as the "Friend" had done, reducing pagination and margins and printing on thinner, inferior paper in order to make whatever savings they could.

People were urged to recycle everything they could lay their hands on, from their precious love letters to cardboard boxes.

Even the children's comics of the time began to carry instructions to their young readers, urging them to add their precious "Beano" or "Dandy" to the pile, telling them they could "Stun the Hun with a paper scrap".

The propaganda was effective. In the spirit of Doing Their Bit, the people of Britain pulled together and rose magnificently to the challenge, increasing the salvage of scrap paper from around 52,000 tons a year before the war to 248,851 by 1940, the time when salvage became compulsory.

By 1942, those neglecting to sort their waste could face up to two years in prison and a fine of £2,500 – quite a daunting prospect at a time when the average man earned only £320 per year! ■

Getty images.

Help put the lid on Hitler BY SAVING YOUR OLD METAL AND PAPER

Families gathered round the wireless to learn how the war was progressing.

Spirit Of The Blitz

Siren Suits

A COSY, one-piece suit is the ideal outfit for wear when sirens sound during winter nights, and the two sketched here are cut on popular and approved lines. Choose a woollen material or flannel and you will be equipped for the chilliest weather.

FOR GROWN-UPS.

SUIT No. 3678 has a front bodice buttoning down the centre with two patch pockets and a neat collar for smart detail. The trousers are joined at the waist, but continue front opening at centre for a little way. One-piece sleeves have shoulder darts and are gathered to wristbands. Hood is made up separately.

This pattern is available in 32, 34, 36, and 38-inch bust sizes. Allow 3¾ yd. 54-inch wide material for 32 and 34-inch sizes and 3¼ yd. for 36 and 38-inch sizes.

TO ORDER.

Paper patterns for the siren suits cost 9d each, post free. To order, please state the NUMBER and SIZE of design wished and your NAME and ADDRESS. Enclose 9d in stamps and send to LIZETTE'S PAPER PATTERN DEPT., "PEOPLE'S FRIEND" OFFICE, BANK STREET, DUNDEE.

No. 3813   No. 3678

FOR YOUNG PEOPLE.

SUIT No. 3813 buttons to waistline and trousers are arranged to button c Hood is attached to neckband and sleeves have cuffs trimming the Patterns are cut in sizes to fit 6-8, 8-10, 10-12, and 12-14 years. For 6-8 ye require 2½ yd. of 54-inch wide material; for 8-10 and 10-12 years, 2¾ yd.; for 2½ yd.

From top tips on making the most of ration packs to a shelter shawl to knit – "The People's Friend" had it all.

IN the darkest days of World War II, the "Friend" took on a new role, making it its mission, with every issue published, to raise spirits and help pass the time in air-raid shelters across the country.

While everyone was aware of the gravity of the situation, they also looked for ways to take their mind off what was going on in the world. So, when the air-raid sirens sounded and folk left the warmth of their homes for the safety of the shelter, many took items to help pass the time.

Along with torches, gas masks and a clutch of important documents in handbags, those organised enough would take a copy of their "Friend" and perhaps some knitting.

An extract from a letter published in 1941 described the scene:

"What amazed me was the number of women folk who were busily knitting as they conversed, while quite a few were engrossed in the 'Friend'. I espied at least half a dozen mothers studying the recipe page. I said to myself: 'What a fine tribute to the 'Friend'.

"Altogether, it was good company to be in, and I certainly never wearied or felt the time lag."

"The People's Friend" offered a bit of comfort in those dark times when no-one knew how long they would be decanted from their homes or, indeed, if they had homes to return to.

Little wonder, then, that the "Friend" also carried patterns for a Shelter Shawl and a Good Luck Tea Cosy, with emblems such as horseshoes and four-leafed clovers.

Any additional luck you could find was welcome, even if you had to make it yourself.

The sharing of tips on how to eke out ration packs was also covered in Kitty's cookery pages with one week focusing on making the most of produce from the allotment.

Among the "Count In Vegetables" ideas was leek pudding and baked cabbage and tomatoes – good enough to rival Woolton pie!

One lady penned a letter to the magazine's "Uncle Jack" saying how she was doing her bit by opening

Children's Corner

Children were catered for among the pages of "The People's Friend", too, where they could follow the adventures of Will and Wag in cartoon strips. The storylines didn't shy away from what was going on in the world around the young reader, with the cartoon strips carrying themes such as "Digging For Victory" and "Socks For Soldiers". One of the tales told of Will and Wag hatching a plan when the home fire was burning low; a little taunting of the coalman achieved the goal of the pair being rained upon by lumps of coal.

"Cousin Tom's Corner" featured stories reflecting the times, including the evacuated cat called Blitz, who was found outside a bombed-out home, while the grown-ups enjoyed the Tweedys cartoon strip, which also allowed a chuckle in the face of adversity, covering everything from the "black-oot" to the Home Guard.

AN OLD TRICK

One chilly morn in winter
The fire Wag went to light,
Of coal there wasn't quite enough
To make the fire burn bright.

With Will to keep him company,
Off in his car he went,
For a grand idea had come to him,
On adventure he was bent.

To the coalman's cart he fixed his car
And shouted at the man,
Who threatened them with lumps of coal,
Which was, of course, Wag's plan.

Women folk were busily knitting as they conversed, while quite a few were engrossed in the "Friend"

her door to a family of eight who had been made homeless as a result of a bomb strike on their house.

She told of one of the girls under her roof reading "The People's Friend", the magazine then being passed around her family for days before moving on to the writer's own daughters.

From there it went to Helensburgh to a sister, then on to London to

another sibling who worked as a nurse in a military hospital.

The trail ran cold at this point, but not before the writer observed "the torture those green covers have to go through". But just think of the many spirits the magazine lifted along the way.

And in the true spirit of the Blitz, "Friend" readers were also keen to do their bit during the war.

The Editor printed a notice under the headline "People's Friend readers help Clydeside air raid victims".

He told of the very warm and practical interest the

readers had shown in the welfare of the children affected, as proven by the magazine's Love Darg appeals.

As well as toys and comforts of all kinds, they had also donated money, ensuring he was able to present £25 to the East Park Home for Infirm Children, Glasgow.

The gesture by the "Friend" readers was all the more generous given how little folk had.

Many people found themselves without a home following nightly air raids, but still the resilience and the spirit of the Blitz shone through.

One letter writer to the magazine told of winning a "Friend" Coronation tea caddy which took pride of place in her home until they had to leave the family dwelling "owing to enemy action".

The back part of the house had been completely wrecked, but when she visited about two weeks later, on top of a pile of debris, she found her tea caddy with the picture of

the King and Queen.

She declared, "It was standing there proudly, just as much as to say: 'We can take it!'"

That fighting spirit was also echoed by the Royal Family when Buckingham Palace was, itself, a target for a Luftwaffe bomber, and the Queen Mother defiantly said, "I'm glad . . . it makes me feel I can look the East End in the face."

One thing that the war undoubtedly did was unify people in the feeling that "we're all in this together".

One letter writer observed – surprisingly, perhaps – that it "has brought love and unanimity among our neighbours that we never before experienced.

"Aways there seemed to be some small grievance that had either to be aired or sulked over. Now, all is changed.

"We live in perfect harmony, each doing the best for the other at all times and under all circumstances and all working for the good of the cause." ■

Wartime Ads That Packed A Punch

Propaganda was a powerful tool during the war years, and advertisers made full use of it to sell their products.

As the war raged on, government campaigns and slogans focused on boosting morale on the home front.

Advertisers were quick to pick up on the propaganda that encouraged patriotism and cleverly turn it to their own advantage.

Slogans such as "Careless Talk Costs Lives" and "Do Your Duty" were used to great effect in the adverts of the era that were carried in the pages of "The People's Friend".

Rinso washing powder placed front-page adverts in the "Friend", embracing the theme of the "Careless Talk" message.

Advertisers also tapped into "Do Your Duty" by declaring new ways to wash clothes that didn't require boiling to get stains out, which would therefore help the war effort by using less fuel – using their product, of course!

Meanwhile Rowntrees Cocoa focused on the life of a busy wartime woman juggling everything from her full-time job to picking up the rations.

Their product, however, promised to "soothe frayed nerves", of which, unsurprisingly, there were plenty.

Wartime was no excuse to let standards slip, however, as Ino Soap declared: "Beauty Is A Duty". ■

ENGLAND EXPECTS

every woman will do her duty

-BY HER COMPLEXION!

Beauty is a duty these days! So simple, too, in spite of lack of beauty aids, for beauty begins with a really clean skin. And that depends more than ever now on your Toilet Soap. INO is pure, fine and super-fatted, with a rich creamy lather that tones and invigorates, nourishes as it cleanses, and leaves your skin youthfully smooth and fragrantly lovely.

Ino *Toilet Soap*

THE FIRST AID TO BEAUTY

"FAIRY'S WHISPER" - Cha

THE PEOP FRIE

THE FAVOURITE HOME JOURNAL

No. 3937—Vol. 119. | Founded in 1869. | JUNE 23, 1945.

Speeches · reports · letters · callers · telephone

—she can never let up

Private Secretary to a busy Member of Parliament—dealing with masses of correspondence — sifting the important from the routine detail — keeping track of her chief's engagements — receiving distinguished visitors — supplying information on a hundred and one subjects at a moment's notice. . . .

An interesting life, certainly, but hard on the nerves. The soothing cup of Rowntree's Cocoa is a great help, she finds; and many a busy housewife will agree with her. Looking after a home, a husband and a family can be one of the most harrying ways of life. From morning to night, ever-

soon gets on your nerves. The children won't get up . . . the boiler fire's gone out . . . there are sheets to be changed . . . the washing-up to be done . . . the rations to be carried home . . . it's raining . . . the dustbin's overflowing . . . you *must* darn the socks . . . you *must* answer those letters . . . you *must* peel the potatoes. . . .

No wonder your nerves become frayed. And no wonder your cup of Rowntree's Cocoa comes as a welcome interlude in such a day; for it calms down jangled nerves and aids digestion. Unlike so many drinks, it contains body-building protein, energy-giving carbohydrate

Founded in 1869. | FEBRUARY 20, 1943. | Registered for Tra by Canadian Maga

WASHDAY "SAVE COAL" SCHEME FOR BRITISH HOUSEWIVES

Target: 1,500,000 Tons a year

NEW WARTIME WASHING METHOD

A SAVING of a million and a half tons of the nation's coal would be made in a year if housewives who boil their clothes every week were to stop boiling! This is true whether women use gas, coal or electricity.

And now here is the new wartime washing method that has been worked out by the Rinso Wash-Testing Laboratories. It gets the clothes beautifully clean *without boiling*. This method requires hot but not boiling water, and only half the amount of water you used to use. The saving in fuel by not lighting the copper is 40 cubic feet of gas if you have a gas-heated copper. Coal users would save 9 lbs. of coal.

How the Method Works

Now the important point, in addition to this colossal saving of coal, is that this way of washing cuts your use of soap by a third, takes far less time and trouble, *and gets the clothes really clean.* Here is the method:

Run off into your sink or wash-bath *half* the amount of water you used to use—slightly hotter than your hand can bear. Sprinkle in *two-thirds* the usual amount of Rinso and

Women all over the country are adopting this wartime washing method.

whisk up. Be sure you have enough water to cover the clothes when they're well pressed down.

Put the whites in first and let them soak for just 12 minutes. Then wash through and rinse. Put the coloureds into the same suds and treat in exactly the same way.

Use the new method for your next wash. Rinso is a No.1 soap powder. 3½d. packet— one coupon. 7d. packet—two coupons.

WASHDAY FUEL-SAVING GUIDE		
National coal-saving target	**10,000,000 Tons** a year	
British housewives' saving (by not boiling clothes)	**1,500,000 Tons** a year	
AVERAGE SAVING PER HOUSEHOLD —ABOUT 5 FUEL UNITS A YEAR		

R 3168-835 | R. S. Hudson Limited.

HEINZ: with its artwork featuring a toy soldier, it proclaimed "Always ready to serve". ▶

◀ **GIBBS DENTIFRICE:** its battledress refill announced it was saving precious metal and was the "patriotic way" to clean one's teeth!

COLGATE: urged us to "Play Safe", tapping into the "Careless Talk" theme of the era. ▶

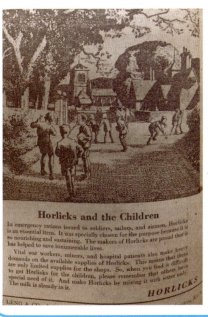

◀ **HORLICKS:** the makers proudly declared that their product had "saved innumerable lives" of Britain's serving men.

Post-War Optimism

Peace had been restored once more, and it was time for the "Friend" and its readers to leave behind the dark days of war and embrace a bright new future . . .

Victory At A Price

With food scarce, tax high and jobs in short supply, the effects of the war would continue to be felt for a few years after its end.

Fashion

1 Test your ankles for weakness. Do it by examining your flatties. If the heels show more wear on the inner or outer rim, you require a strengthening exercise.

2 Without shoes, walk five minutes daily on the borders of the feet; on the outside borders if heel wear on inside, on the inner borders if heel wear on outside.

3 Whether or not your ankles are weak, practise walking. Place heel lightly on floor, immediately roll weight through the foot and "grip" shoe sole with toes. You'll soon be walking as though high heels were part of you!

THE war was over, and the country was moving slowly towards an age of prosperity. This would be the era of Harold Macmillan's "never had it so good" speech. The welfare state was created, the economy eventually regained strength and some countries saw full employment levels.

First, Britain had to rest and heal. One letter from a reader in Ayrshire in 1945 showed the important part the "Friend" played in those years.

"Now the wars are over, may I write and thank you for the excellent editorial notes you have written about these wars from time to time.

"Being a woman, I know nothing of war. Your weekly notes explained much to me that I could not have understood. You were ever sure of victory and, even when disaster threatened, wrote so hopefully that one was always cheered by your views.

"Just as you wrote about the war itself you often wrote of its problems, shopping, queuing, prices and all the other things that have bothered housewives. As a housewife and a woman I send you my thanks!

"Being a woman, I know nothing of war. Your notes explained much to me that I could not have understood"

"I just hope you will be as successful in advising us about peace problems, and what we can expect."

The "Friend" was certainly not shy of speaking out against what it saw as injustice. Just after the war, an editorial laid out reasons why families might no longer feel they had a home in this country.

With high taxation and bureaucratic barriers to starting a small business, folk were looking at the colonies for a living.

Soldiers had visited better places or heard about them while at war, meeting other soldiers who came from New Zealand, Canada and the like and told them about the need for skilled labourers and the opportunities available in these blossoming economies.

In one politically charged piece, the "Friend" commented on its hopes for the Budget in 1949.

"In recent months more and more goods have appeared in the shops and stores. Yet their appearance doesn't bring them any nearer to the people in most need of them.

"Prices remain exorbitant. Goods are still

1946-1950

Dec 1946
The beloved Christmas film "It's A Wonderful Life" opened in cinemas. It starred James Stewart.

Dec 1946
President Harry S. Truman delivered Proclamation 2714, which officially ended hostilities in World War II.

Nov 1947
Princess Elizabeth, soon to be Queen Elizabeth II, married Philip Mountbatten at Westminster Abbey. The bride was attended by eight bridesmaids and two pageboys. On the morning of her wedding, Princess Elizabeth snapped her tiara. Thankfully the royal jeweller was on standby and was escorted by police to Buckingham Palace.

July 1948
Health Secretary Aneurin Bevin launched the National Health Service to provide free healthcare to all in Britain.

WELCOME HOME

The British spirit would pull people through, but things would get worse before they got better.

marked at two or three times their pre-war value, with no corresponding increase in their quality.

"If he is alive to the deadly effect of high taxation, the Chancellor of the Exchequer has a glorious opportunity very soon to deal with it boldly and realistically. He can do it by abolishing one tax – the Purchase Tax."

As the magazine reached eighty years old, it was called "The People's Friend: The Favourite Home Journal", and still cost only 2d.

"What Other Folk Do" was one popular feature. Subjects included a lady who lived in Barrie's House, Kirriemuir, and a chapper-up, who used a

wooden club to knock at doors till he got an answer.

Others included a maker of tawses (straps), of which the "Friend" said: "Opinions, of course, differ widely concerning the use of the tawse, but Mr Dick regards it as a friend to the teacher."

Another job unique to the time was the Tinkers' Padre, who went out into the countryside to find people in their tents and offer his services.

"I admired the glory and beauty of the setting sun on Machrihanish Bay, and told myself, as I watched silently, that the setting sun could scarcely shed its golden glimmer on a more moving sight than the Tinkers' Padre at work.

"William Webb is their minister, adviser, lawyer and guide in all things. He laughs with them, and weeps with them. He writes their letters, signs their documents and settles their disputes.

"He is a man with a big heart, for he is a man who loves humanity."

The spirit of the people would pull Britain through, but things would get worse before they got better.

Food became scarce in 1946 – wheat in the west, rice in the east – and the "Friend" declared that this new famine was the arrival of the fourth horseman of the apocalypse.

The other three – disease, war and death – had clearly already been

here for the last eight years.

It was hard to believe that only a year or two before, food had been so plentiful that it was burned for fuel in locomotives.

One reader made a lovely observation about national spirit that offered a more optimistic view of things to come.

"Have you ever noticed how beautiful the colours of the Union Jack appear against a dark and overcast sky?

"Is this not symbolic of the people of this grand old island? When things are really black, is this not our shining hour?"

And so it would prove, as life slowly returned to normal. ■

Aug 1948

Twelve-year-old jockey Lester Piggott won his first-ever race at Haydock Park Racecourse.

March 1949

Laurence Olivier's "Hamlet" became the first British film to win a "Best Picture" Oscar.

June 1950

The first mass holiday package tour was when Vladimir Raitz, co-founder of the Horizon Holiday Group, launched charter flights between Gatwick and Corsica. Before long Brits were going abroad to Palma. The first holiday in 1950 cost £32 10s and you even got a meal on the propeller-driven, war-surplus Dakota transport plane, which, after a refuelling stop at Lyon, deposited you six hours later at Calvi, Corsica.

Dec 1950

The Stone Of Destiny, the coronation stone of monarchs, was stolen from Westminster Abbey by some students.

Looking To Better Times

The country bore the deep scars of war, and at last thoughts could be turned to rebuilding Britain's devastated landscape.

POST-WAR optimism was wearing thin in the early years after the war ended.

The promise of better times ahead was slow to materialise and rationing was still having a big impact on households. Bread wasn't taken off rationing until 1948 – and it was to be a few more years still before meat and bacon rations were relaxed.

The cookery pages in the "Friend" offered achievable recipes given the constraints of the ration books, and "egg-free" Easter recipes ensured that something could be put on the table, including Mock Marzipan Eggs and Hot Cross Buns – using dried egg, of course.

Even competition prizes in the magazine reflected the wants of its readers.

One letter writer complained, "It is a sad

The tide of change was gathering momentum and plans progressed to improve housing

reflection on the times we live in that after nearly 2,000 years of civilisation, women have to go about bare-legged." It was fitting, then, that the "Friend"

offered nylon stockings as prizes during this time.

The Festival of Britain in 1951 did, however, give the nation something to look forward to. It was a showcase of all things great about our country – the event was said to be a "beacon of change" and it helped lift the sombre mood caused by austerity.

"The Festival of Britain

has proudly sent out its invitation to the rest of the world," the "Friend" proclaimed, adding, "on the south bank of the River Thames is housed examples of British workmanship, ingenuity and skill . . . let us be good hosts."

The tide of change was gathering momentum, and plans progressed to improve housing. It was the chance to rebuild Britain's devastated landscape and create modern housing and a new way of life that people craved.

One reader from Glasgow pointed out, "The first item in educational progress must be the wiping out of slumdom. Finer homes in a more

Let The Games Begin!

London hosted the 1948 Summer Olympics – known as the Games of the XIV Olympiad. The 1940 and the 1944 Games had been cancelled due to WWII.

Fifty-nine countries took part in the Games, though both Germany and Japan were excluded.

iStock.

1951-1955

Jan 1951
"The Archers" was broadcast nationwide for the first time. "The everyday story of country folk" is still going strong.

March 1951
Cheeky comic character Dennis The Menace first appeared in the "Beano". Children and adults still enjoy his capers!

A Beano Studios Product © D.C. Thomson & Co. Ltd 2018

Feb 1952
George VI died aged fifty-six at Sandringham House. Known as Albert until his accession and "Bertie" to his family, he was never expected to be King, but due to the abdication of his brother, Edward VIII, he was thrust into the role.

Dec 1952
The Great Smog blanketed London. It caused traffic chaos and up to 4,000 deaths.

congenial atmosphere is the best foundation for the training and guidance of our future citizens."

Architects were keen to put into action their plans for modern living. People wanted housing better suited to their needs, and although prefabs helped ease some of the country's

New towns also sprang up around Britain – among them Stevenage in England and Glenrothes in Scotland

immediate needs, they weren't intended to be a lasting solution.

"The appearances of the houses are very ugly," one reader visiting South Shields commented on the prefabs. "They are mostly erected on old coal tips. If they were painted a nice colour, instead of the cold, dingy, grey white, I think they could be made to look quite attractive."

New towns also sprang up around Britain – among them Stevenage in England and Glenrothes in Scotland.

A reader sent in a picture of a ten-storey modern block of flats which was Glasgow's answer to the housing problem: "It looks like a sky-scraper, but is

A New Era In The Royal Household

It was an era of change for the Royal Family. Britain mourned the death of King George VI, who died on February 6, 1952, aged just fifty-six.

The "Friend" commented, "How unexpectedly the pattern of life can change. A dearly beloved King has passed to his rest and his gracious daughter has been proclaimed Queen.

"The impact of these historic events – the stunning news of the King's death; the cancellation of the Royal tour of Australia and New Zealand; the sad home-coming of a brave young woman to take over the heavy responsibilities of Queenship – can still be felt . . .

"Transcending all things one fact is clear – life goes on. A new reign begins, a new chapter in the long, proud history of Britain and the Commonwealth opens."

The following year, in June of 1953, the country united in celebration of the Coronation of Queen Elizabeth II.

Of the event, the "Friend" Editor said, "It opened in a blaze of almost unparalleled glory . . . the solemnity and dignity of the occasion, coupled with all the rejoicing and thanksgiving have left a mark on all of us", adding, "Never has the Crown been so firmly secure in Britain; never has the Royal Family enjoyed such popularity and respect."

very comfortable to live in," she said.

Perhaps Britain now had reason to enjoy post-war optimism – the birth of the NHS created a new era in healthcare, where there was the promise of being cared for "from cradle to grave", as well as the far-reaching benefits of the discovery of the structure of DNA.

Though things were changing, one thing remained constant – "The People's Friend" – and its loyal readers were quick to share opinions and thoughts.

One poignant letter came from a "Survivor Of The *Titanic* Disaster":

"As a Glaswegian by birth, may I say how much I enjoy Jennie Cairns' great story 'Grey River Flowing West.'

"As I read this week's instalment, I wondered if any other reader could make the claim to having been among the 711 rescued from the *Titanic* disaster.

"Although I was quite young, I can still remember the experience. I lost my father in the tragedy, but I was one of those picked up by the *Carpathia* and her gallant crew.

"Four years ago, while on holiday at a little fishing village on the east coast, I had the pleasure of meeting the skipper of a fishing boat who had been one of the crew of the *Carpathia* at that memorable rescue.

"I visited his home and saw the medal presented to the *Carpathia's* crew in appreciation of their gallantry." – N.H.P., Glasgow. ■

March 1953
Tommy Taylor, the twenty-one-year-old centre forward, became Britain's most expensive footballer in a £29,999 transfer from Barnsley to Manchester United.

June 1953
Princess Elizabeth became Queen Elizabeth II after her Coronation at Westminster Abbey.

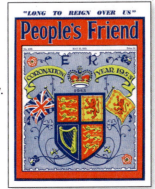

May 1954
Roger Bannister became the first person to run a mile in under four minutes – three minutes 59.4 seconds to be exact! He managed this with minimal training while practising as a junior doctor. Bannister's record only lasted 46 days when it was broken by his rival, John Landy.

July 1955
Ruth Ellis became the last woman in the United Kingdom to be hanged. She had been convicted of murder.

Britain On The Move

With rationing over and a new monarch on the throne, Britain's progress was entering a whole new era.

RATIONING ended in 1954, and with the war now well behind us, the country moved forward apace.

As the cookery pages of the "Friend" reflected, the spread of available foods was widening. Ready meals began to make an appearance, with an advert for a Kraft macaroni cheese meal that took just seven minutes to make.

The five-day working week was now commonplace, but "there are many who don't like it," we reported.

Too much time, and what to fill it with? The "Friend" warned against joining the crowd "who find enjoyment in mass adulation" of the movie stars and rock and roll icons of the time.

There was still much satisfaction to be found in getting involved in your local community, spending time in your own company and practising traditional arts and crafts that were in danger of being left behind in an era of "mass production and uniformity".

"Friendship multiplies joys," an article declared, and companionship should never go out of fashion no matter what was changing in the world.

Driving became

1956-1959

Feb 1956
Doris Day recorded one of her most famous songs, "Que Sera, Sera", from the film "The Man Who Knew Too Much".

April 1956
Hollywood star Grace Kelly married Rainier III, Prince of Monaco.

Sept 1956
The hard disk drive was invented by technology company IBM. This was the very first "storage device" for computers!

April 1957
The United Kingdom agreed to give Singapore its independence after being controlled by Britain since 1824. It had been a trading post of the British East India Company and was occupied by Japan during World War II.

affordable for most people, and folk were now able to travel to the country and seaside for weekends and holidays.

Some country roads became a little busy, but motorists were soon to find some relief as the first motorway was built (the M6), shortly followed by the M1 between Watford and Birmingham.

Whether you were heading to a caravan in Wales for the weekend or flying to America for a holiday, the era of true mass-market travel

There was still much satisfaction to be found in getting involved with your own community

had begun.

While the international market was growing substantially – the "Friend" featured adverts for European destinations from Spain to Norway – holidays at home were still popular.

This was the era of the holiday camp. Billy Butlin first had two hotels in the Bahamas, but from 1953 onwards he opened one hotel after another in the UK, promising entertainment for the whole family for just a week's pay.

In 1956, the Suez Crisis was a defining moment for Britain. It was clear the country was no longer the global authority it once had been, and the time seemed to have come for a more wholesale dismantling of the empire.

"The old country is facing a crisis," the "Friend" declared. "Sometimes it is easy to lose heart and be tempted to join in the theory that this country is finished. Stormy weather lies ahead. We have faced similar conditions before today. We can face them again."

A number of colonies gained their independence after the war, from India and Pakistan to Malaysia, Ghana and the Sudan, while the flow of Brits to Canada and Australasia was constant. Letters coming in from overseas showed the spread of readers, from Rhodesia to Saskatchewan and Tasmania.

In these countries, change had been even quicker for the residents than it was in Britain.

"To the people of the British Isles, one hundred years of history may not mean much. But a great deal has been accomplished in that time," a reader from British Columbia wrote in the province's centenary year.

Infrastructure, housing, industry – no wonder the "call of the colonies" was so strong, as these places now offered a standard of living comparable to anything found in Britain. But the pace of change was about to speed up in the "old country" as the 1960s dawned . . . ■

THE "FRIEND" DOCTOR TALKS

SURGERY

The Friendly Doctor

Ten years after the NHS began, the "Friend" started "The Doctor Talks" column, and addressed some of the pressing healthcare concerns of the time.

Studies have shown that children in the 1950s often ate better than today's children, with high-fibre foods, low sugar intake and more vitamins coming from vegetables rather than fruit.

So a lot of the major diseases that troubled parents in the early part of the century were gone, and the worry was more about what the pace of modern life was doing to adults.

Of that adult advice, there was often a clear split amongst advice between the sexes. Men were prone to over-eating and could be less conscientious about following a course of medicine.

Women, on the other hand, had to be careful not to over-

stretch themselves. This was a special concern considering that "it's a fact that women do have more energy than men."

The good news was that, as medicine advanced, the list of conditions that could be treated without an operation grew.

As claims of slimming qualities began to appear in adverts for eggs and other foods, we advocated common sense.

"If you're within a stone of the weight shown for your height and age, you've nothing to worry about. I don't advocate fancy diets. A gradual, fairly easy process is better."

It was important that husbands step up and chip in at home, with help in the evening, not walking too fast ("there's no pleasure in always trying to catch up with a man's long stride") and making the Sunday breakfast.

Every little helped!

June 1957

The very first Premium Bond winners were selected by the computer ERNIE – Electronic Random Number Indicating Equipment.

Dec 1957

The Royal Christmas message by the Queen was broadcast on television for the very first time.

Jan 1958

Godtfred Kirk Christiansen filed a patent for the iconic plastic Lego brick. The company would go on to produce 400 billion Lego elements.

iStock.

Aug 1959

The original and stylish Mini, designed by Sir Alec Issigonis, was launched in Britain. This most recognisable of cars came about because of a fuel shortage caused by the Suez Crisis.

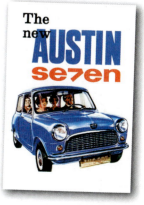

The new AUSTIN se7en

Alamy.

On The Cover

On June 2, 1953, at the age of twenty-five, Elizabeth was crowned in Westminster Abbey, and the country celebrated.

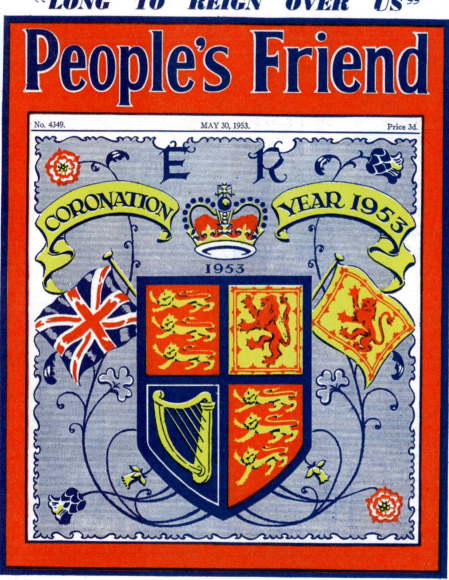

May 30, 1953

This spectacular cover reflected the wave of wellbeing overwhelming the nation. War was past, and though rationing was still to end, the country had peaceful times ahead.

"Glorious June has gone. But it will be long before it is forgotten. It was a month when history was made and austerity had no place."

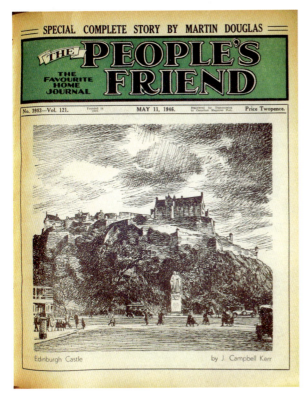

May 11, 1946

The first pictorial cover featured Edinburgh Castle.

Nov 10, 1951

A sweet portrait of the heir to the throne.

Oct 9, 1954

This vibrant cover was a break away from the norm.

Dec 21, 1957

This Christmas issue contained extra pages.

The 1950s kitchen featured a whole host of exciting new gadgets and appliances.

The Era Of The Housewife

With hire purchase terms on gadgets to lighten the load, this was a great time for the busy woman.

THE 1950s is often described as a golden age. The war was in the past, sugar finally came off rationing, and household gadgets came into their own.

The "Friend" advertising pages carried a parade of appliances all guaranteed to lighten the load of the housewife, especially for spring cleaning – or, as it was called in one March editorial, "The Annual Upheaval".

"Round about this time the pleasant, comfortable atmosphere of home-life is disturbed. For a few days at least, everything will be topsy-turvy. Meals will be of a rushed and scrambling variety; tempers will be slightly frayed and general chaos will reign."

Did the husband take any part?

No, this was something which was apparently relished by the housewife.

"She sees beyond the upheaval. Not for herself is this annual spring cleaning tackled.

"It's for her family and home. To give it new life and sparkle; to add to its warmth and cheer."

A poem by "Friend" favourite Edgar A. Guest entitled "When Mother Is Away" summed up the man's role in its final lines:

"Homes are sorry sights to see when they're left in charge of men,
And there'll be no order here until she returns again."

Still, the 1950s housewife could take comfort in the fact that she wasn't expected to do this alone. No, indeed!

According to the advertisers, there were 101 appliances and gadgets designed to make life easier, and all available on hire purchase.

"The new gas washing machines will do the week's

wash in next to no time. And a gas drying cabinet will dry it all in less than an hour ready for ironing."

"The Hoover electric washing machine saves hours of hard drudgery every week."

"The Jackson Electric Cooker is recommended for ease, economy, cleanliness and perfect cooking. And no Purchase Tax added!"

"For quicker, easier spring cleaning get a new Hoover cleaner. Does so much more than ordinary vacuum cleaners."

"You will like the new Ewbank carpet sweeper for its lighter, easy control."

So was the housewife's day really full of drudgery? Well, it certainly was heavy. Even the "Friend" doctor advised caution

And, of course, piggybacking on the washing machines came the detergent ads – Persil, Daz, Surf – all guaranteeing the whitest wash.

So was the housewife's day really full of drudgery? Well, it certainly was heavy. Even the "Friend" doctor advised caution.

"Monday is the most dangerous day of the week. It's washing day, and that means I'll have a sprained wrist and sprung tendon to deal with.

"It happens when a housewife tries to make her wrists do the job of a wringer. They twist far too vigorously and snap goes a tendon.

"Housewives are tired and that's when accidents happen.

"Try to take five minutes'

Golden Days

Letters at this time would seem to suggest that, though they felt fortunate when comparing the work of their grannies' daily lives, readers looked back on those days with fondness . . .

"Just now my thoughts turn towards the washing of blankets. How I treasure my mother's old wooden five-legged peggy and wringing machine with wooden rollers. Despite the magic of the modern electric washer there's a lot to be said for the old way.

"Into the tub go my blankets. Round and round I work my peggy among the soapy suds. Then up goes a blanket into the wringing machine's wooden rollers. Twice through the rollers for each blanket and it is ready for hanging out of doors."

"As a child my mother wore a holland "brat" to keep her dress clean. Later she wore a linsey apron to do her dirty work and a pure white linen one for baking. On Friday nights she always wore a clean

print to signify that the week's work was done.

"Girl workers now wear nylon overalls which are washed out in a few minutes and are ready to wear when dry!"

"My dearest possession is my mother's spinning-wheel. As I look at it my mind goes back to my childhood.

"I see the cosy kitchen in a lighthouse cottage and the big range with a glowing fire. Tea was past and we children watched as Mother got out her wheel.

"Then came the familiar whirr, whirr, whirr as she

got busy.

"Later as I lay in the big kitchen bed I could still hear the murmur of the wheel until it lulled me to sleep.

"I often wish I'd learned to spin. I remember how Mother washed the Shetland wool, teased and carded it with a drop of oil, then formed it into rolls ready to start the spinning and make the strong two-ply wool.

"This was made mostly for Father's socks. No other wool kept his feet so warm during a long watch in the cold light-room."

break between jobs."

The doctor had more home truths to give.

"One of the most common causes of accidents is the tin opener. And be careful when using steel wool to clean out pots. If a strand gets under the nail it can get infected."

He even warned about not lighting the gas cooker properly.

"Many women turn on the gas before they have the match or taper ready. And if she's at the cooker several times a day, can you wonder that she's below par in the evening?

"Any time your gas doesn't light at once, be sure to go to the door or window and have a few deep breaths of fresh air."

The new improved methods weren't restricted to gadgets and appliances, however. Batchelor's advertised their chicken noodle soup – "just like Grandma's". In foil sachets, it cost 3d a plateful and took just seven minutes to make!

Meanwhile the Twink Home Perm promised "soft, shining curls for you from now till Spring".

Proof that the 1950s

housewife had some leisure time, however little, can be seen in the proliferation of home shopping catalogues.

Littlewoods promised that this "thrifty, save-up way is the modern, common-sense way of shopping."

"Earn an extra wage packet every week in your spare time," Kays cried. "No limit to spending, and highest commission paid."

Wouldn't our grannies marvel, could they return for just an hour to see what help their granddaughters have these days in getting through the chores? ■

Ardrossan Town Hall   J. Campbell Kerr.

Old Burgh Buildings, Stirling   J. Campbell Kerr.

A Brush With J. Campbell Kerr

The front cover paintings of British beauty spots have been one of the best-loved parts of the "Friend" since the 1940s – but the identity of the artist has long been shrouded in mystery.

HE'S a man that many people over the years claim to have met, or even to be distantly related to. But in fact, there has never existed an individual christened J. Campbell Kerr who has produced cover artwork for "The People's Friend".

The name is an alias, a brush name used over the years by a small group of talented artists who have created the unique illustrations for the front cover of the magazine in the distinctive J. Campbell Kerr style.

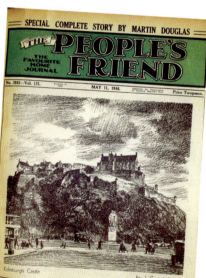

The story begins in 1946, when the "Friend" featured its first front cover to show an illustrated scene of a Scottish beauty spot – Edinburgh Castle.

It appeared with no fanfare or fuss on the May 11, 1946 issue, and though there was a short paragraph inside paying tribute to "Edina! Scotia's darling seat!" there was no mention of why a scene had suddenly replaced the advertisements that until then had been ever present on 1940s front covers, nor of the artist who had produced it, though the byline "J. Campbell Kerr" was prominently displayed.

It was an innovation that proved an immediate hit with readers.

"The etching of Edinburgh Castle was beautifully done, and J. Campbell Kerr is to be congratulated on a splendid piece of work," M.S. of Edinburgh wrote. "The new cover seemed to give additional dignity and

A Chance Encounter

Many years ago I had the honour and pleasure to meet Mr J. Campbell Kerr, the artist who produced many of your front page covers of your magazine, hence the following story.

I was on my way to school, in the local village, Comrie, in the early 1950s, when J. Campbell Kerr asked me if I had anything suitable at the farm he could sit on whilst doing his artwork. A wooden lemonade crate was found and dropped off behind the stone dyke we had pre-arranged as a hiding place.

Sadly the crate was not strong enough and was found behind the dyke with a note attached: "Could not take the strain", signed J. Campbell Kerr.

Mr A.D.

There was no mention of why a scene had suddenly replaced the advertisements that until then had been ever present on 1940s front covers

richness to the 'Friend', and is in keeping with the fine traditions of your magazine."

Interestingly, later that same year, front cover illustrations with the credits Ian Ramsay (who illustrated the magazine's first English cover scene, a view of Regent's Park, London, on issue dated August 3, 1946) and C.F. Green interspersed J. Campbell Kerr's offerings. These were most probably freelancers brought in to supplement gaps perhaps arising from staff holidays or illness, but it quickly became the custom for all cover illustrations to be credited J. Campbell Kerr, regardless of who had created them.

The confusion around J. Campbell Kerr's identity seems most easily explained as follows.

It's not unreasonable to assume that some of the artists who painted the front covers fell into the habit of introducing themselves as J. Campbell Kerr as a kind of shorthand way of explaining what they did for a living – in much the same way that actors who have played the same character for a long period of time might be just as well known by the character's name as their own.

The small band of J. Campbell Kerrs has included some of the finest Scottish artists, male and

Portrait Of The Artists

From 1946 up to the 1980s, the vast majority of the artists illustrating under the J. Campbell Kerr name were D.C. Thomson staff members, based originally in the Bank Street Art Department, and then later, in the Meadowside Art Department.

Many of them continued with the work even after leaving the company to pursue freelance careers.

Peter Davidson remembers those days.

"I was a Bank Street artist in the early 1960s. Jimmy Reville sat behind me – he is the long figure, upper left, in the drawing.

"He illustrated the 'Friend' covers every week until he retired. On a technical note, when Jimmy drew the covers, he painted the sky in bright blue on a separate sheet of acetate paper, and painted the bottom half on illustration board. How methods have changed!

"Alf Anderson, who I think was Norwegian, sat to my left. He drew the black and white

story illustrations for the 'Friend'. He was a nice man who used to share his cheese sandwiches with me every morning.

"I have fond memories of that time. It was the best apprenticeship any budding commercial artist could have had."

Also in the drawing, in the bottom left corner, is Norman Lee, another popular and prolific J. Campbell Kerr who went on to illustrate short stories and serials for the "Friend" well into the 1990s.

female, of the 20th century. Many of their names remain elusive, hidden for ever by the alias.

Douglas Phillips, who was also responsible for creating the illustrations for the much-loved "The Farmer And His Wife" series, was one of the longest-serving and most prolific of the artists to work under the brush name, contributing over 1,000 cover paintings.

Gilbert Dunlop, born in Alloa in 1909, was a particularly illustrious J. Campbell Kerr. He joined the staff of D.C. Thomson in 1927 at the age of eighteen, and attended evening classes at

Dundee's art school.

"He had a natural talent," his granddaughter Joanna Murray once said. "But he never boasted about it; he just got on and did it."

Over his long career, much of which was spent as a freelance illustrator, he created artwork for Enid Blyton, designed greetings cards for Valentines of Dundee, and worked extensively for "The People's Friend" and other D.C. Thomson titles. He passed away in 1984.

But why did the Editor of the 1940s "Friend" settle on the name J. Campbell Kerr? We can only speculate, but the choice may have been influenced,

consciously or unconsciously, by one of the most famous and highly regarded Scottish artists of the mid 20th century.

James McIntosh Patrick, who was born in Dundee in 1907 and studied at the Glasgow School of Art, was elected a member of the Royal Scottish Academy in 1957. In the 1930s, he was producing many highly detailed landscape oil paintings of scenes in and around his native Dundee and the Angus countryside.

Perhaps it was hoped that a little of the great man's glory might be reflected upon his fictional counterpart? We will never know for sure. ■

A Corner For The Children

The Children's Corner was a regular feature of the "Friend" for over a century, with stories, puzzles and general knowledge for the little ones.

By 1913 Cousin Tom's Red Book League had over 1,000 members. In 1918 each 10th new member received a prize – if a boy, a knife; if a girl, a needlecase.

Those of my cousins in the League promise:-

(1) To love and obey my parents, and do all I can to help them.

(2) To respect my teachers and learn my lessons as well as I can

(3) To be kind and obliging to my schoolfellows and friends

(4) To be kind to animals

FROM the start the "Friend" was intended for the whole family, from youngest to oldest, and the Children's Corner was a page dedicated specially to the younger members of the family.

Early amusements for children included acrostics, stories and riddles, often quite challenging ones.

In 1908 Uncle Jack, then in charge of the Happy Home club, made a pointed request to the Editor.

"I hope a large number will compete in our Domestic Servant competition. I may even be able to persuade that hard-hearted man, the Editor, to give me a whole page of the "Friend", if my nephews and nieces back me up strongly enough!"

Later that year a new page appeared – Boys And Girls Own Page – and immediately afterwards there was a new relative,

AT THE PANTOMIME

Cousin Tom. Just as Uncle Jack begged his nephews and nieces to write to him, so the children became cousins to their very own Cousin Tom.

The new children's page was lively, with pictures,

poems and things to make.

There were stories of heroes, both fictional and real, alongside competitions, puzzles and snippets of general knowledge for those eager to learn.

WILLIE WADDLE AND WAG.

Wag threw the fish to all the cats,
And said. " Now, please go 'way !"
The cats just grinned and miowed at him—
" With you we're going to stay !"

The shouts and threats of our poor friends
Were not the slightest use.
" What fools we were," said Wag to Will,
" To let this army loose !"

At last they reached a river bank,
With fear the cats all whined.
Our friends dived in and swam across—
The pussies stayed behind !

During World War I the "Friend" did not shy away from the topic.

In 1914 the children learned to make a paper Dreadnought and could play a game called "Pot Shots At The Kaiser".

Since German toys were no longer in favour the Children's Page had projects for home-made wooden toys, and featured stories of heroism such as "True To His Cause, the story of a brave Belgian Scout".

A cartoon panel depicted the adventures of a range of characters before a certain duo made their debut in 1929.

"Next week a new and exceedingly funny pair will make their appearance in our Corner. Their names are Willie Waddle and Wag. Will is a duck and Wag is a dog, and they are the most comical pair you ever heard of."

Will and Wag went on to have hundreds of adventures, accompanied by a growing cast of family and friends in Wagtown.

In the Forties the pair collected scrap metal for the war effort, while sixty years later they were attending aerobics sessions and signing up for computer classes.

Readers loved Will and Wag so much so that the "Friend" printed a pattern for a jumper depicting them in 1987.

The Children's Corner remained a mainstay of the magazine until 2016, but Uncle Jack, Cousin Tom and Will and Wag will always hold a special place in our hearts. ■

Though the appearance of this mischievous pair changed dramatically down the years, their ability to get into scrapes – though unwittingly – provided plenty of material for adventures.

The Adventures Of Will And Wag

April Showers

As they walk past Auntie's house,
The lads see no-one there.
The front garden is empty
And the flower-bed is bare.

They've gone to post a letter,
But it soon begins to rain,
So Will and Wag take shelter
Till they walk back home again.

Passing Auntie's house once more
The bed's now full of flowers.
Up pops Pete and says,
"The April showers brought the flowers!"

Changing Times

The Sixties and Seventies were defining years for Britain, transforming the country into a place of freedom and hope, and the "Friend" was there every step of the way.

Role Model

Princess Margaret was a young woman in 1960. Like many readers, she had lived through the war, making her a popular role model for young wives of the time.

It was in August of 1960 that the Scottish-born Princess Margaret celebrated her thirtieth birthday – an event the "Friend" marked with these words:

"A Royal Princess born to an enchanted Scotland –

Our thoughts went out in love, sweet homage paid.

Now, charming, beautiful, gay and endearing,

She holds our hearts in willing thraldom still,

And lovingly rejoicing in her gladness

We wish her every gift Life has to bring."

Swinging Sixties

Optimism for the future was at the forefront of the minds of the "Friend" and its readers.

AS the Sixties dawned, the "Friend" had to keep up with the rapid changes the decade brought. A new generation had arrived, and with it growing incomes, new fashions, music and changing social attitudes.

It was 1960 that saw the end of conscription for husbands, fathers and brothers of British women, and the pages of the "Friend" began to focus on young wives and mothers, and their families and homes.

Being a good wife and mother was important to the female readers, with much of the magazine's content focusing on fashion, cookery, household tips and women's health – not least the adverts, which were crammed full of corsets, laundry detergents and Crimplene yarn!

In those post-war years, women wanted to look their best, and beauty tips appeared in a regular feature called "Beauty Brief".

With advice on how to disguise dark circles, apply eyeliner and keep your hair moisturised, the "Friend" of the 1960s had something for every young woman of the time.

Keeping a clean and orderly house was

Advances in technology in the 1960s dramatically changed how people spent their leisure time

important, and advice on spring-cleaning was often featured. As the Editor wrote in 1961, "Let's be honest! Is there a woman who doesn't love every moment of the self-imposed task of spring-

cleaning?" These few words summed up what was expected of a woman in the early Sixties, but not all of the readers agreed!

One, a Mrs A.M. from Lisburn, wrote to the Editor, complaining about her husband.

"Why is that whenever we have visitors, my husband becomes the perfect gentleman?" she asked. "Nothing is too much trouble for him. He even helps me with the washing-up! Yet when we are on our own he never lifts a finger to help."

From 1962 the "Friend" began a regular feature focusing on DIY, urging women to pick up a paintbrush or learn to lay linoleum, and in 1963 a new series began for newly married couples setting up home together.

Advances in technology in the 1960s dramatically changed how people spent their leisure time.

Households started to become better off, and many people bought cars and other consumer goods, such as TVs, washing machines and refrigerators.

1960-1964

March 1960
The Vietnam War began. It saw America sending 3,500 young men to fight.

Alamy.

April 1960
"Ben-Hur" won a record-breaking 11 Oscars. It had been nominated for 12 in total.

Alamy.

April 1961
Cosmonaut Yuri Gagarin became the first human in space. His Vostok spacecraft made a complete orbit of the planet Earth. He died in 1968 when the Mig-15 training jet he was piloting crashed.

iStock.

May 1961
Hollywood favourite and humanitarian George Clooney was born in Lexington, Kentucky.

A new series began in 1963, helping young couples to set up a home of their own.

With television ownership becoming more widespread, TV was the medium of the age in the 1960s, yet many newsworthy events remained unreported in the "Friend".

This was in keeping with its original pledge in 1869 that nothing would appear in the magazine that would "corrupt the morals of either old or young".

By the mid-1960s, with more families now owning their own car, the freedom to holiday further afield was enjoyed by many, and features in the magazine mirrored this.

Advice on how to pack a suitcase, pick a caravan site and survive a long road trip were all suggested to "Friend" readers.

The Editor himself gave some fundamental advice: "During the next few weeks thousands of people will be meeting for the first time . . . Get talking to them. Get to know them and you'll be amazed how much they reflect your own lives. It doesn't matter how far you travel, ordinary folk are the same the wide world over."

People holidaying in Europe became more commonplace, which was evident in the cookery pages.

Cookery expert Elizabeth Craig began treating readers to recipes for European dishes such as gnocchi, pizza, risotto and croissants.

Edgar A. Guest's poems were a regular feature in the magazine during the Sixties, despite his death in 1959.

Born in Birmingham in 1881, he moved to Detroit in 1891. After he left school he joined a Detroit newspaper, and in 1916 he began writing at least one poem a day until his death.

One of his poems, "Always Faithful", was published in the "Friend" in 1964.

"I look at my shelves of books and say

Here are my friends for a rainy day;

Always faithful and always true

No matter what I myself might do,

Here they are ready and neat and trim

Always on hand for my slightest whim."

The "Friend's" cover paintings have always been recognisable, though in the 1960s they were very different from today's, exclusively featuring urban scenes of Scottish cities and towns. The cover was the only part of the magazine to be in colour.

The black and white pages meant that Alex Muir's new gardening column, which began in 1966, wasn't able to feature garden photos.

Instead, readers were urged to get outside in the fresh air, look after their gardens and see the world for what it really was – an inspiring place with bright prospects for the future. ■

Aug 1962

Hollywood superstar Marilyn Monroe was found dead in her Brentwood home. A certain amount of mystery still surrounds her death.

Feb 1963

The Beatles recorded their debut album "Please Please Me" at Abbey Road Studios.

Nov 1963

President John F. Kennedy was shot and killed during a visit to Dallas. There has been endless speculation ove the years as to who was responsible, even after the arrest of Lee Harvey Oswald.

Sept 1964

The Forth Road Bridge was officially opened over the Firth of Forth.

Britain In Transition

Some big changes were coming, for the country and for the "Friend" . . .

AS the Sixties continued, the pages of the magazine were filled with stories and features depicting the changing times.

It was in 1967 that the "Friend" published its first "trouser suit" paper pattern – a big change from the neat skirts and dresses previously offered – and the cookery pages were filled with recipes from around the world.

In 1968, the UK saw the first woman to be appointed First Secretary of State, and the Women's Liberation Movement was beginning to make headlines. In 1970, the Equal Pay Act came into force, which prohibited unfavourable treatment, in terms of pay and employment conditions, between men and women.

In 1968, the idea of women proposing to their partners on February 29 was discussed by the Editor after receiving many letters from readers asking about

In 1969, "The People's Friend" celebrated its 100th birthday and a special centenary tea towel was available for readers to buy

Subsequently, the pages of the "Friend" carried a series by Margaret Nicol about a "Lady Postie" – a job that had until recently been exclusively for men.

this tradition.

In his reply, the Editor stated, "Scotland can claim the honour of being the first country to make it legal. An Act was passed by Scottish Parliament during the reign of Queen Margaret."

He then added, "Perhaps Miss 1968 has no regrets that she didn't live in those faraway days. She is much better off, enjoying a freedom, independence and equality that were beyond the wildest dreams of her fair ancestors."

In 1969, "The People's Friend" celebrated its 100th birthday and a special centenary tea towel was available for readers to buy.

The Editor had a few words to share on the subject.

"Today, after a hundred years of unbroken publication, 'The People's Friend' enjoys a unique

Just For The Kids

Cousin Tom's page was a wealth of news and information for children. A regular feature focused on special stamps from around the world. In the run-up to a US election, a stamp was released of Abraham Lincoln in 1965 to mark the centenary of his death. But this wasn't an American stamp – it came from Rwanda in Africa!

1965-1971

Dec 1965
Spacecraft Gemini 6 and Gemini 7 performed the first controlled rendezvous in orbit.

July 1966
England beat West Germany 4-2 in the World Cup Final.

Jan 1967
Donald Campbell was killed during his attempt to break the water speed record on Coniston Water. His rocket-powered boat, *Bluebird*, began to bounce on the surface while travelling at 328 mph, resulting in a cartwheel. Campbell died on impact. His body was eventually located on the lake bed in 2001 and he was laid to rest in Coniston Cemetery.

April 1968
Martin Luther King Jnr. was shot and killed in Memphis, Tennessee.

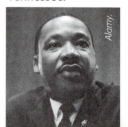

place in the hearts of the reading public . . . We, who are privileged to carry on the good work started by others, are ever grateful to readers old and new. Their support, loyalty and unfailing encouragement throughout the years has been a source of inspiration to all."

How true those words are to this day!

Soon after this, metrication was introduced to the UK, and several full-page notices from the

Shortly before decimalisation began on February 15 the price was still given as 6d, with 2½p in brackets following it

Metrication Board began to appear in our pages, giving advice on how to measure in centimetres.

For people used only to using imperial measurements, they advised: "You'll be surprised how much more confident you feel about metric measuring when you've tried it yourself."

This was followed not long after by the introduction of decimal currency in the UK in 1971.

The first "Friend" issue of

On The Bright Side!

The most significant change to "The People's Friend" was when it began to be printed partly in colour in 1970. Printing in colour was now cheaper and more readily available than it had been before – and what a difference it made!

Until now, the front cover scenes had mainly been of towns and villages, but the new colours available meant that more scenic illustrations by J. Campbell Kerr were now visible on the news-stands.

Fiction illustrations were given pride of place, often taking up an entire page, and were much more stunning and eye-catching than the black-and-white illustrations of old.

Colour pages didn't just brighten up the magazine and make it more pleasing to look at; they allowed for a wider range of features to be included within.

With many families now owning a camera, readers were urged to send in their snaps for inclusion in a new feature called Snap Happy, where photos of family members and pets took centre stage.

Those lucky enough to have their photos printed were rewarded with a prize of two guineas, and the feature was a favourite among "Friend" fans, continuing until around 2012.

With readers now living in a world of colour TVs, hand-held cameras and foreign holidays, life in the early Sixties seemed much more than a mere decade ago!

the year, dated January 2, 1971, was priced at 6d. Shortly before decimalisation began on February 15 (light-heartedly referred to as D-Day in the magazine), the price was still given as 6d, with 2½p in brackets following it.

With money on the mind, holidaying in Britain was still the preferred choice for many Brits, and the magazine's features, giving advice or inspiration for "holidays at home", sat amongst adverts for caravan holidays, coach holidays and ferries to here, there and everywhere in the British Isles.

However, travelling abroad was increasingly easier for families, with many forgoing their annual trip to the coast, instead opting to holiday in Spain or Malta.

Even the Rev. T.R.S Campbell had taken to the skies, wondering at the miracle of flight in his column.

On reaching an altitude of 30,000 feet, he enthused: "It was unbelievable! In this tiny world of ours, we were like gods on high and on wings swifter than the eagle's."

The "Friend" doctor had something to say on the subject, too.

"Perhaps you are flying abroad and are rather nervous about flight. Well, please don't worry. Remember that you are far more likely to have an accident within sight of your own home than you are in a plane."

The "Friend", its readers and contributors had reached new heights, and the future was looking very bright indeed. ■

July 1969

"The Eagle has landed." Neil Armstrong stepped out of the lunar module and became the first human to walk on the Moon.

April 1970

Britain's Maggie Smith won the Best Actress Oscar at the Academy Awards for her role as an unrestrained teacher in the film "The Prime Of Miss Jean Brodie". The film was adapted from the book by Muriel Spark. Maggie Smith went on to play another well-known Scottish teacher – Minerva McGonagal in the Harry Potter films.

Dec 1970

Paul McCartney filed a lawsuit against the other Beatles members, ending the band for good.

Aug 1971

Frederick Forsyth's gripping novel "The Day Of The Jackal" was released. It tells the story of a professional assassin hired to kill Charles de Gaulle. Forsyth himself worked for MI6 for over 20 years, using his career as a writer to gain access to political leaders.

118

During the 1970s more English scenes began to feature on the front covers.

A New Chapter

"The People's Friend" was a constant in the lives of readers, who were experiencing a very different Britain from the one they had known.

IN the Seventies, the "Friend" enjoyed a unique place in the hearts of its readers, and despite many changes, it remained the same in its aim and beliefs.

Wholesome stories, blended with romance, highlighted the best in human nature, and every story and feature published

in the "Friend" carried an uplifting message of good cheer.

This was evident in a new reader feature which appeared regularly in 1973 and 1974 and was entitled "Together Again". Readers were encouraged to tell their own stories of unusual or unexpected reunions.

Many happy tales were

shared, including one of a husband returning from war to meet his child for the first time, and another of being reunited with a missing pet.

One unusual anecdote told of a lady having been pulled over by the police for speeding, recognising the officer as an old friend, and inviting him to tea!

In 1972, readers were treated to beautiful colour photography of the Queen's silver wedding aniversary. This coverage was supplemented by a specially written serial for the occasion, "So Gladden Our Days" by popular author Jennie Cairns.

As the Editor wrote in the November 15 issue,

1972-1979

Aug 1972
The Tim Rice and Andrew Lloyd-Webber musical "Jesus Christ Superstar" made its West End debut.

March 1973
The Watergate Scandal occurred. It would eventually lead to the impeachment of President Richard Nixon.

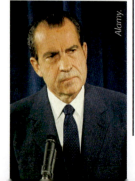

March 1974
The Three Day Week came to an end at last. It had been introduced by Prime Minister Edward Heath to limit the commercial use of electricity to three consecutive days each week. The British economy was troubled by high rates of inflation, and pay caps saw industrial action taking place.

June 1975
"Jaws" was released in cinemas, making everyone scared to go into the sea!

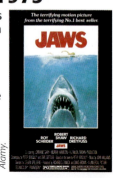

"Wedding anniversaries are always occasions not only for celebration and well-wishing, but also for casting lingering sentimental glances back down the years that have been shared together.

"When an entire nation and Commonwealth claims the couple as their friends, then there's no doubt a great many people will be looking back as the Silver Wedding of the Queen and Duke of Edinburgh draws near."

Inspired by the experiences of the

The magazine still had a distinctive Scottish feel to it – in its fiction especially

characters in her serial, Jennie Cairns invited readers to contribute their memories of when events in their own lives coincided with milestones in history to a series called "And On That Very Day".

From around 1973, despite the fact that, since 1971, all cigarette packets were required to have a health warning, cigarette advertising was plentiful in the "Friend", taking up entire pages on occasion.

As fashion evolved and brighter and more garish colours began to creep into wardrobes across Britain, so they did on the pages of

the "Friend". Sometimes it was necessary to look twice to distinguish whether or not the bright swirls belonged to clothes or to the wallpaper behind!

During the Seventies more English scenes began to feature on the covers, but despite this, the magazine still had a very distinctive Scottish feel to it – in its fiction especially.

"And Flourish Together", a story by Jean McDougall, was specially written to celebrate Glasgow's 800th birthday in 1975.

For the Queen's Silver Jubilee in 1977, the Editor took the opportunity to look back over the last 25 years.

"Twenty-five years ago comparatively few people could either afford a television set or lived in an area where the TV signal could be received.

"Travel is no longer the prerogative of the few. Surely the additional breadth of understanding gained by seeing different people, places, ways of life, either in another corner of the British Isles or farther afield, can be no bad thing.

"Communication today is probably better than it's ever been – communication between employer and employee, between husband and wife, between nations. There is often disagreement on whatever is discussed, but at least it *is* discussed."

As the decade drew to a close, the installation of Margaret Thatcher in 1979 as Britain's first female Prime Minister made the future seem more exciting and forward thinking than ever before, moving into a new chapter in the story of Modern Britain. ■

The World Of Work

Life was changing fast. The Sex Discrimination Act came into force on December 29, 1975.

In 1976, the "Friend" contained advertisements from the newly formed Equal Opportunities Commission to say how some things would change as a result.

Astonishingly, until 1976, banks, building societies and finance houses had been allowed to discriminate against women – refusing access to mortgages, loans and other forms of credit or offering them on much worse terms than those available to men.

Many also demanded that a woman provide a husband, father or other male relative or friend to act as guarantor for any product she was allowed to take out.

As well as equality of opportunity in employment, the law now required these and other businesses to offer their products and services on equal terms to men and women.

The adverts in the "Friend" soon began to reflect the changes – addressing women as people in their own right.

Building society Abbey National was quick to invite women to apply for their services with an advert reflecting the many and varied roles that female employees were now carrying out in the workplace.

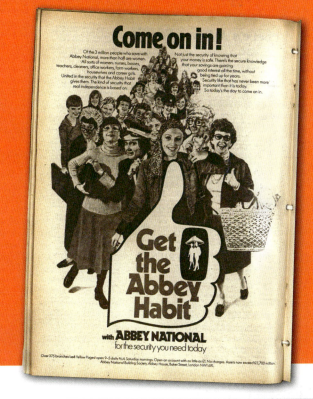

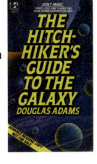

On The Cover

As the "Friend" approached its centenary the tides of revolution –
social, musical and political – swirled around it . . .

Bargain Pattern: A SUMMER FROCK FOR BIG SIZES

THE
PEOPLE'S
FRIEND

No. 4760   APRIL 15, 1961   PRICE 4d.

Crieff

J. Campbell Kerr

April 15, 1961

The magazine witnessed the changing face of Britain and the wider world with equanimity.

"Come what may, the old fundamental truths and qualities will remain constant. There will always be a place for goodness and beauty, for family life and the links that bind it together."

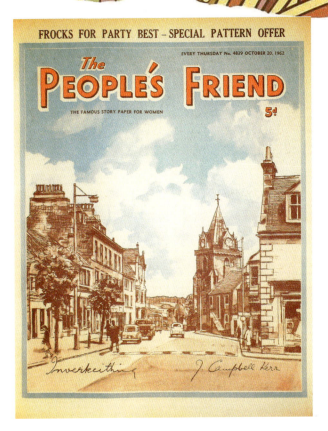

Oct 20, 1962

The "Famous Story Paper For Women" cost fivepence.

April 3, 1965

The psychedelic era seemed to have bypassed Wick.

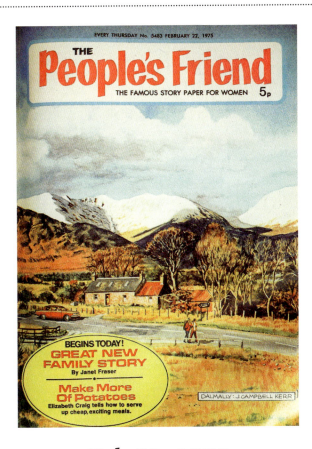

Feb 22, 1975

Good, old-fashioned food was on the menu here.

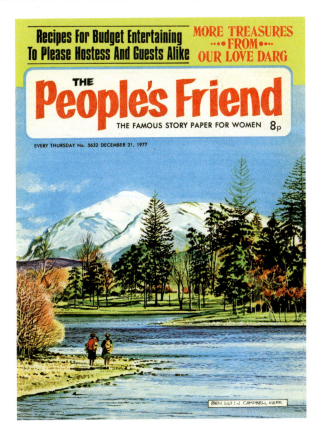

Dec 31, 1977

We rounded off 1977 with a peep at the Love Darg.

With his pet parrot, Basil.

FROM 1958 the "From The Manse Window" column was written by someone who would go on to do so for twenty-seven years.

Thomas Robertson Strathern Campbell, better known as T.R.S. to the staff and to his parishioners, was the beloved reverend of St Andrew's Parish Church in Dundee, also known as the Trades Kirk.

St Andrew's Church has a long association with the Nine Trades of Dundee.

In 1770 the Trades and the Kirk session petitioned the town council of the time for the erection of a fourth church. When the council refused, they decided to erect the church on their own account.

T.R.S. enjoyed his chaplaincy to the Trades, and on his death in 1985 they paid tribute with a window in the church. His parishioners did the same.

In his articles for the "Friend" his warm nature and strong belief endeared T.R.S. to readers. His love of animals was a regular topic, like this comment on the constancy of dogs:

"There is a lesson to be learned from the dog.

"He takes life as it comes, glad for your attention be it great or small, concerned only to be your ever-faithful friend. If we could add that to our natures it would be in us a God-like attribute.

"A friend ever loyal, ever constant, ever, ever faithful. What better could we be?"

As well as writing for the

The People's Minister

For over a quarter of a century, "Friend" readers were uplifted weekly by the cheerful and encouraging words of Rev. T.R.S. Campbell.

Tributes flooded in from readers.

...was sorry to read the sad news of the passing away of the Rev. T. R. S. Campbell. I always read the editorial first followed by Rev. Campbell's wonderful, uplifting article.
— Mrs M. McD., Muir of Ord.

He was a very inspiring man and helped many, I am sure, along life's highway.
— Mr J. S., Bury.

May God bless Mr Campbell now he has gone to be with his Lord whom he served for so many years, and bless the family he has left behind.
— Mr and Mrs C. M., Doncaster.

The messages he gave so faithfully each week were greatly appreciated and looked forward to.
— Miss N. A., Blackburn.

Three years ago I had the privilege of going to St Andrew's Church while on holiday with thirty other ladies from the W. I. in Ireland. We were all kindly welcomed to the service. Afterwards the Rev. Campbell talked to us all and came outside so we could get some photographs, which made our trip to Dundee a memorable one.
— Mrs D. McG., Strabane.

Many of his writings have been cut out and enclosed in letters to friends and family at home and overseas, and we keep a "treasure-box" of his articles which are read and re-read.
— Mr and Mrs R. R., Reedley.

I started reading the "Friend" as a child growing up in Buckie and now have my subscription sent to California. The Rev. Campbell's column always meant a lot to me and I appreciated his wisdom and common-sense outlook on life. You were so right in saying that he gave many the courage to go on. This was specially true for me since I was born with cerebral palsy.
— Mrs M. T., Berkeley, U.S.A.

WE were very moved by the number of letters we received following our announcement of the death of the Rev. T. R. S. Campbell, B.D. Here is a small selection of the tributes paid by readers to this well-loved man.
— Editor.

Although I never met him I felt I knew him well.
— Mrs A. P., Blaenau Festiniog.

His writings were so sincere and very helpful for they spoke of everyday conditions in everyday life.
— Mrs I. M., Bolton.

My husband, mother and I were very sorry to read of the death of the Rev. T. R. S. Campbell. He was indeed a very great man and a talented one.
— Mrs M. McI., Ellon.

Mr Campbell's simplicity and compassion and his closeness to Jesus made him a true disciple indeed.
— Miss W. P., Glasgow.

My regret is that I've never been to Dundee as I always promised myself I would go to hear his service and would have loved to shake his hand. Through the years he has given me great comfort.
— Ms A. W., Berwickshire.

He made Christian faith and the practice of Christian virtues a part of everyday life.
— Mr M. L., Leeds.

He will be missed so much by so many people, like myself, who looked forward each week to his articles, which were so very true and helpful.
— Mrs F. O., Rochdale.

I felt I had lost a dear friend.
— Mrs D. M., Ravenstonedale.

How sad I felt when I read of the death of the Rev. T. R. S. Campbell. I have always treasured the friendship he has given to us all during his long association with "People's Friend."
— Mrs P. S., Leeds.

What a wonderful gift he had, sharing his faith and giving cheering messages to readers for twenty-seven years.
— Miss D. S., Bridlington.

It was with deep sorrow... Rev. Campbell's passing... thanks to God for his life and work. The members of our church, St Andrew's United Reformed Church, Wallheath, are currently creating a rose garden round the church and we intend to donate a tree to his memory.
— Mr and Mrs G. H., Kingswinford.

We have lost one of the men we can ill afford to lose, someone who helped, guided and inspired thousands of people.
— Mrs M. R., Swansea.

For many years I have enjoyed his contributions to your magazine, and at times I have used them as devotions for our church group.
— Mrs J. W. T., Niagara Falls.

His article was the first thing I would look for and read each week. He had a wonderful way of writing his lovely message.
— Mrs D. S., Milford Haven.

A few years ago I went with my son to spend a few days in Edinburgh and while there I said we must go to Dundee and find the church and hope to see the Rev. Campbell. Being complete strangers it took us a little while to find the church, but the Rev. Campbell wasn't there, so we went to his house and how welcome we were made.
— Mrs R. H., Plymouth.

magazine, Rev. Campbell wrote and directed plays, and was an authority on Rabbie Burns. He was also a golf fanatic, and assiduously collected the autographs of some of the world's finest golfers.

His parishioners thrived under his care. Present church elder of St Andrew's Ron Chimiak recalled laughing helplessly on first hearing T.R.S. giving his talk to the children one Sunday.

"My father-in-law, who was with me, was not amused with my laughter, but by the end of T.R.S.'s address he, too, was laughing!"

In 1974 T.R.S. wished readers a happy New Year:

"Most Sundays over the years I have said something for God and Christ, and have never used an old sermon. I know my theme is inexhaustible, and every Sunday I attempt to make the Word a living Word.

"Should the day ever come when I feel I have nothing fresh to say, then I will know I have become old."

That day never came. ■

▲ The Trades window is in the east gallery. It depicts the church, the old Howff graveyard (appropriately, since long ago each trade would hold meetings at the grave of a departed member), and the Trades Hall.

▶ The Word window sits in the gallery to the east of the organ. It was created by artist Douglas Hogg on the theme of Agnus Dei, the Lamb of God, and reflects T.R.S.'s life and ministry.

Followers Of Fashion

The "Friend" designed its own paper patterns for dressmaking, which readers could order through the pages of the magazine.

THE paper patterns sold through the "Friend" were designed by the team in Dundee and were popular with dressmaking readers. Sometimes they were teamed up with fabric packs offered as competition prizes. During WWI when paper was rationed, a diagram was sent instead, which readers would scale up to create their own template.

Early pen sketches were replaced by colour in the Fifties, before photography was introduced in the Sixties. The models were ordinary women, typical of "Friend" readers. Ann Meiland, one of the Sixties models, recalled, "I was in the park one day when I was approached and asked if I would be interested in modelling. It was a fun thing to do when I was a young mother." ■

● By 1961 the full skirts of the Fifties were giving way to fitted sheath dresses and suits finishing just below the knee. Even in an illustration, the well-dressed lady would still step out with hat and gloves in place.

● By the mid Seventies maxi skirts were everywhere. Worn on many occasions, they featured strong, bold fabrics which previously might have been considered better suited as home furnishings. Look closely and you will see the skirt almost matches the carpet.

● With dinner dances and formal dining popular in 1973, a long dress was essential. This one was made in a patterned chiffon fabric typical of the time, but keeping those "cape-style" sleeves out of the soup must have been difficult!

● The fashion for women wearing trouser suits was well established by the time this outfit appeared in 1971. Captioned as suitable for casual or formal wear (but still too early for work wear), it features wider-legged trousers, a nod towards bell bottoms.

A Friend In The Kitchen

Elizabeth Craig was the "Friend" cookery editor for many years, providing tasty recipes that changed with the decades.

BEFORE Nigella, before Mary Berry, before even Fanny Craddock, there was Elizabeth Craig. A daughter of the manse from Angus, Elizabeth was very much the celebrity cook of her day.

She was born on February 16, 1883, one of eight children. Her parents, Rev. John Mitchell Craig and Catherine Nicoll Craig, lived in the village of Memus, just north of Kirriemuir. Elizabeth attended nearby Forfar Academy, where she later returned to teach.

But journalism beckoned, and in her twenties, Elizabeth joined the staff at D.C. Thomson in Dundee, the publisher of "The People's Friend" and local newspapers such as the "Dundee Advertiser" and "Dundee Courier". Here she began her almost 70-year association with the "Friend".

Growing up in a large clergyman's family in rural Scotland, Elizabeth learned the virtues of thrift and household economy.

Writing later, in the introduction to one of her many cookery books, she credited her mother with providing this early domestic education.

She certainly proved an apt pupil. For when her career took her to London, her skills in the kitchen saw her rise swiftly to become the most in-demand cookery editor on Fleet Street.

After her marriage to American war correspondent Arthur E. Mann in 1919, Elizabeth became a freelance writer, keeping her family name for professional purposes.

Her recipes were published in newspapers and magazines up and down the country, and her reputation as a food expert was growing. In 1923, she published the first of more than 40 books.

It was unusual in days gone by for staff writers to be given bylines in their publications, and so much of Elizabeth's early journalism for the "Friend" and for D.C. Thomson's newspapers is no longer identifiable as hers.

Later, as she became established as a freelance writer, editors were eager to let readers know that the famous Elizabeth Craig was writing for them.

And write she did! Her contributions to magazines and newspapers over the decades were prolific.

In addition to writing, she was also something of a celebrity, appearing on radio and television programmes, and making personal appearances and performing cookery demonstrations up and down the country.

She continued her association with the newspapers serving her childhood home, with reports on weddings in the area, such as a column headed "Pretty Society Wedding – Distinguished Guests' Gowns Described" in the "Courier" in July 1919, and of the Royal Family's sojourns to Scotland – "Mayfair Moves North" – in August 1924.

She was publishing many well-received booklets and pamphlets of recipes. Some she wrote on behalf of food companies, demonstrating how to use their products in imaginative ways.

In addition, lucky "Friend" readers were treated to a number of recipe collections by Elizabeth Craig, given away with selected issues of their favourite magazine.

The quantity of recipes Elizabeth shared with "Friend" readers was prodigious. Always

In addition to writing, she was also something of a celebrity, appearing on radio and television programmes

produced with an eye to economy, the themes altered over the years to reflect new ingredients that became available with growing post-war trade.

In 1973, when Britain entered the Common Market, Elizabeth produced features about recipes from European countries for readers to enjoy. She also reflected the increasing availability

A Good Personal Friend

80th birthday.

In the issue dated August 9, 1980, the Editor paid tribute to Elizabeth Craig in his letter to readers:

"Many readers may have already heard about the recent death of Elizabeth Craig who wrote our weekly cookery feature for so long.

"Her loss is a sad one for everyone here who knew and worked with her. We have lost not just a valued contributor, but a good personal friend.

"Elizabeth Craig was in her ninety-eighth year and she was first associated with the "Friend" almost seventy years ago. This was a unique accomplishment, but then she was a truly unique woman.

"[She] was never happy if she wasn't working, and one of the last items she wrote for the 'Friend' was a typically distinctive contribution to the feature which we published last week to mark the Queen Mother's

"Sadly, now she is gone, and I am sure readers will share the great sense of loss we all feel. Quite simply, there was no-one like her, and she enriched the lives of everyone she met."

of labour-saving devices in the kitchen and in ingredients she was able to add as time-saving shortcuts for busy readers.

She was writing for everyone, though in the Sixties and Seventies, her recipes were aimed mostly at busy working women with young families to feed.

Mindful of the lack of time, as well as tight budgets, she provided quick, easy dishes that would be tasty and inexpensive with features such as "Five Day Menu For Working Wives", "Desk Top Dining" and "Freezer Treats".

Clearly recalling the lessons from her mother so long ago, in 1978 she produced a mini-series for young wives. Starting with "Happy The Bride", featuring a gorgeous two-tiered wedding cake, the series went on to make up a beginner's cookery course over the next four weeks.

Though she had no children herself, she had a good understanding of what children enjoyed. Well into her nineties, her cookery features included "Meals For The

Youngsters", celebration cakes for children's parties, and even a number of features teaching children how to cook.

"Let's Start Cooking" featured "Children's Corner" favourites Will and Wag, and Elizabeth's encouraging introduction:

"Here are some scrumptious treats to make yourself. You'll find it's great fun and quite easy if you follow the instructions carefully, but ask Mum's or Dad's permission first."

With only a little supervision in the kitchen, children were encouraged to make meals that made enough to feed four, giving

them a real sense of accomplishment. She also advised them to "try to leave the kitchen clean and tidy when you've finished cooking." A good lesson for everyone!

Elizabeth Craig remained a valued contributor to the "Friend" throughout her career. She died on June 6, 1980, at the age of ninety-seven.

In 1980, the average time taken to produce an issue of the magazine was three months, so her final contributions were on the news-stands some weeks after her death. Her final cookery column appeared in the August 2 issue. ■

Modern Times

During the Eighties and Nineties, young women looked to strong female role models to guide their ambitions. The "Friend" was there to encourage readers in every sphere – and to uphold the importance of home and family.

130

TAKE YOUR PARTNERS AT THE **TROPEZ**

Nine To Five And Beyond

Technological and social changes made themselves felt in the Eighties, but the "Friend" remained a constant, reassuring presence no matter what.

Over To You

The "Friend" always valued the conversation it had with its readers.

Letters pages had been included since the beginning, but once the magazine started to include colour pages, there was scope for so much more.

Readers began to share their pictures and stories as never before. So rich and varied were the contributions that they were turned into a number of regular series which began to run in the magazine.

Joining "Snap Happy", the Eighties saw several popular new series featuring readers' letters and photos, such as "Happy Event", "Then Their Dreams Came True", "Women In Khaki", and "Dance In The Old-fashioned Way".

The latter was inspired by the popular fiction serial "Take Your Partners At The Tropez", which ran in 1987.

THE options for women were expanding rapidly by the time the Eighties began. Legislation in the Seventies had opened up opportunities in every field, and by 1979 Britain even had its first female prime minister in Margaret Thatcher, who remained in post throughout the decade.

With a woman as head of state and now another at the head of government, there were plenty of role models for young women making their way in life.

The number of women entering the workplace – and staying there after getting married and having children – was rising. This was the age when women seemed to be on the way to "having it all". They could have a successful career and a successful home life – or so the story went.

The "Friend" reflected the trend in working wives with more recipes for busy families who didn't

necessarily eat together.

Elizabeth Craig, ever mindful of her readers' needs, produced recipes for one "for those times when you find yourself eating alone", as well as dishes suitable for children and some lovely celebration cake recipes.

Working mums often reported feeling guilty, and spending time in the kitchen with the children was Elizabeth's way of enhancing those precious hours.

This was also the decade the microwave oven began to make its way into domestic kitchens for the first time. Elizabeth Craig died in 1980, but the new cookery editor of the "Friend" began featuring recipes for this shiny new gadget, also geared to saving time through the working week.

In a 1982 cookery feature, she said, "When it comes to saving time and energy, a microwave cooker is an investment that's hard to beat. Handy though they may be for

speedy defrosting of frozen produce or throwing together a quick snack, there's much more to the microwave than you think . . . So get switched on to the 1980s and try some of our speedy recipes."

Social changes were making themselves felt, too. For the first time there were holidays for single-parent families, activity holidays for young people away from their parents as well as holidays specifically for disabled people in our annual holiday guide in 1981.

It was a decade of royal weddings. Prince Charles married Lady Diana Spencer in July 1981. Readers inspired by the royal couple were treated to an eight-page pull-out feature on how to plan a wedding.

Readers also sent in their own wedding photos to "Snap Happy" and "Between Friends", while the magazine featured the wedding venues and royal residences associated with

1981-1988

July 1981
The wedding of Charles, Prince Of Wales, and Lady Diana Spencer took place at St Paul's Cathedral.

April 1982
The Falklands War began when Argentina invaded the Falkland Islands.

July 1983
English actor David Niven died aged seventy-three. Niven appeared in many films both before and after a successful military career. Some of his famous roles included "A Matter Of Life And Death", "The Pink Panther", "Around The World In 80 Days" and "Raffles".

Feb 1984
Torvill and Dean won gold for their incredible "Bolero" performance at the Winter Olympics in Sarajevo.

the couple, as painted by J. Campbell Kerr.

Almost exactly five years later, Prince Andrew married Sarah Ferguson in July 1986, marked by a series of lovely features in the magazine on the couple and the wider royal family.

Women's fashions were changing. Perhaps inspired by American TV hits such as "Dallas" and "Dynasty", shoulder pads were all the rage. In the mid-Eighties, it wasn't unusual to see "executive women" with a severe case of shoulder-pad build-up, with blouse, jacket and coat all adding to a look that was more American footballer than office wear.

The magazine's popular paper patterns were more restrained in their fashion recommendations; pretty dresses and smart trouser suits were more in keeping with readers' preferences.

In times of such rapid change, the "Friend" was a reliable constant. The familiar mix of readers' letters, favourite places, recipes, knitting and craft, together with reassuring advice from the "Friend" doctor, was a constant weekly pleasure.

John Taylor and his wife, Anne, on the Riggin also made their debut in this decade and quickly became firm favourites. In 1989 a Canadian reader wrote to the letters page with a picture of her parents in Alberta, which she called "The Farmer And His Wife". Seen on their tractor, Mum and Dad were still farming their own 320-acre farm, and John and Anne were the family's favourite part of the magazine.

Readers wrote to the magazine in their

This was the age when women seemed to be on the way to "having it all"

hundreds. The Editor noted in 1983, "As well as from all over the British Isles, we get letters from many countries on the African continent and, as you can imagine, from America and Canada and Australia and New Zealand.

"Soon after the Falklands crisis was over, readers from that part of the world renewed their links with us. If you're a newcomer to the 'Friend' please drop us a line. We'd love to hear from you. I'd like to think you, too, could become a friend

and join our worldwide family of readers."

Perhaps strangely, this was almost the only mention of the 1982 Falklands conflict that appeared in the magazine, reflecting the Editor's policy that the "Friend" should remain a refuge for readers and never a source of worry or concern.

Throughout all the changes brought by the decade, nature was always there to provide interest and wonder. Nature writer Anne Deacon provided a monthly countryside column which, with its beautiful illustrations, was a winner with readers, and inspired several versions on the ever-popular "Friend" calendar tea towel.

As ever, the "Friend" never lost sight of the fact that it was people and the relationships between them that really mattered.

As the Editor said in his preview of the 1985 Diary: "We've chosen the theme 'Meet People, Make Friends', and that includes readers who aren't able to get out and about easily. Readers with time to spare are sure to find at least one address of interest out of the many charitable organisations we've mentioned in the diary . . ." ■

July 1985

Super concert Live Aid took place in both London and Philadelphia.

Jan 1986

Space Shuttle Challenger disintegrated 73 seconds after launch, killing all seven astronauts on board.

Oct 1987

The Great Storm of '87 was caused by a cyclone. The areas most affected were Greater London, the East Anglian coast and the Home Counties, and over 15 million trees were felled. It's most remembered for TV weatherman Michael Fish telling us, "Don't worry."

Feb 1988

The first ever Red Nose Day raised an amazing £15 million for charities at home and abroad.

Bright New Days Ahead

The digital age beckoned, and on the eve of a new millennium the "Friend" reflected upon the century it was leaving behind . . .

THE "Friend" has never been the home of the latest celebrity gossip. It has, however, included people in the public eye who are in tune with readers and their values.

Much-loved personalities such as Harry Secombe, Thora Hird and Val Doonican graced its pages in the 1990s, with a warm blend of anecdote and humour about their long and eventful lives in the entertainment business.

Well-loved TV programmes had their place, too, particularly "Take The High Road", "Tales Of Para Handy" and "Dr Finlay", with series going behind the scenes of all three over the decade.

It was a turbulent decade for the royal family, who featured regularly in the pages of the magazine. Robin Johnston's series

"As it always has, the 'Friend' belongs to you. Your letters, your pictures, the stories and memories you share with us are all-important"

celebrating the Queen Mother's ninetieth birthday prompted a huge postbag of readers' memories of "the nation's

grandmother", which ran for several weeks.

Readers' memories were also a rich source of interest and information about days gone by. Mrs J.T. of Morecambe, in her letter to the "Women In Uniform" series, told us about her time with the

Danesbury Dough Bashers who made the Army's bread during the war. Her letter appeared alongside that of Mrs G.D. of Birmingham, who had been on duty at the Military Hospital during WWI and recounted some of the harrowing scenes that she had witnessed.

Those ladies were typical of a generation who had served with good humour and dedication in whatever capacity they could to see their country through a time of national crisis, and the "Friend" was proud to feature their memories in its pages.

The "I'd Like To Know" page remained a favourite. A fair sprinkling of the letters reflected the changes that developments

Nobody's Perfect!

● The "Friend" is, of course, passionate about accuracy. However, staff are human, so the (very) occasional error did and does slip through from time to time. The Editor is always grateful to people who get in touch with constructive criticism, like this reader

who contacted the title in 1991 . . . "In a recent issue of the 'Friend' it was stated in 'I'd Like To Know' that Paul Daniels married Debbie McGee in July 1987, which is untrue. The actual date was April 2, 1988 – and I should know! – Debbie McGee."

1990-1999

June 1990
Joanne Rowling, or J.K. Rowling as we know her, had the idea for Harry Potter whilst on a train from Manchester to London.

Feb 1991
British scientist Tim Berners-Lee introduced the WorldWideWeb while working at CERN in Geneva.

Dec 1992
During her Christmas message, the Queen described this year as her "annus horribilis". It was a tumultuous year for Her Majesty that saw her son Prince Andrew separate from the Duchess of York, Princess Anne divorcing Mark Phillips, Charles and Diana separating and Windsor Castle being badly damaged by fire.

Jan 1993
Bill Clinton was sworn in as the 42nd President of the United States of America.

in technology were making to communication.

"Everyone seems to communicate by fax these days," Mr J.P. of Solihull wrote. "I wondered who invented the fax and when." The Editor was able to tell Mr P. that Alexander Bain had patented the first such machine in 1843!

Changes were also in the mind of cookery writer Lee Millar after "Metric Day" (October 1, 1995).

"Well, it's about a month since the 'Friend' went metric," she wrote. "I must admit, it's not as difficult as I thought it would be . . ."

She went on to explain that the "Friend" recipes would henceforth be published only in metric, with a conversion chart to accompany them, "to help you convert your old favourites".

This was one change that didn't stick, however, and a few years later, recipes were once more printed with quantities given in both metric and Imperial.

It had been a decade of change. It began with conflict both at home and abroad, as the poll tax riots and the war in Kuwait dominated the 24-hour news cycle. Britain grew closer to Europe as the Channel Tunnel opened, and further away as we left the European Exchange Rate Mechanism.

Despite all the various disagreements, there was a sense of optimism in the air by the end of the decade, reflected in the soundtrack to the 1997 general election, "Things Can Only Get Better".

In keeping with its mission to entertain and not alarm readers, and with its political neutrality,

Our Home Town

The Nineties were an exciting time for Dundee, which celebrated 800 years since it had received the charter that made it a Royal Burgh.

To mark the occasion, the "Friend" ran a specially commissioned serial.

"Next week," the Editor wrote, "you can start reading a superb new Story that follows the fortunes of one Dundee family from the end of the last century to the present day. 'The River Calls Us Home' is written by a favourite 'Friend' author Betty McInnes – who just happens to be a local lass! – so adds a wealth of authentic detail to a compelling Story full of memorable characters."

The story became one of most popular of all the "Friend" serials, and – uniquely – was repeated by popular demand in 2009 for the 140th anniversary.

In addition, we highlighted several of the many women of achievement associated with the city.

● Mrs Keiller, inventor of Dundee marmalade.
● Fanny Wright, daughter of a Dundee merchant, born in 1792, who became an anti-slavery campaigner in America.
● Lady Jane Ogilvie, who founded an orphanage and convalescent home in the city.
● Miss Mary Baxter, who founded Queen's College, and went on to become the first Chancellor of Dundee University when the college became independent of St Andrews University, to which it had been affiliated.
● Mary Slessor, a Dundee weaver who became a missionary worker in Nigeria and is remembered for her tireless efforts to secure women's and children's rights.

Here, as ever, the "Friend" celebrated brave, dedicated women whose lives left the world a better place.

the "Friend" refrained from comment on the turbulent events of our times, but one tragedy had to be reflected in its pages.

The death of Princess Diana in 1997 moved the world to tears. Even those who had not been her greatest admirers were filled with compassion for a promising life cut short, and for the two motherless princes she left behind. In the week of her memorial concert, there was a special eight-page tribute to the princess and her legacy.

On a more cheerful note, 1999 saw the magazine looking back to days gone by and forward to an exciting new millennium.

"This is our 130th birthday issue," the Editor said in his letter. "It's the mixture as before; something to be proud of, in our case. The best of stories – fascinating articles about favourite places – all the regular writers you like so much – and, of course, yourselves. Because, as it always has, the 'Friend' belongs to you. Your letters, your pictures, the stories and memories you share with us are all-important."

Anticipating the bright new millennium, we offered readers a number of souvenirs. There were products such as the year 2000 tea towel, craft items to make, including a millennium sampler, and special features such as "A Century Of Cooking".

In the final issue of that year, there was a promise to readers: "Next Week The 'Friend' Welcomes In A New Millennium With A Bright New Look".

There were exciting times ahead. ■

Mar 1994

Steven Spielberg's powerful film "Schindler's List" won seven Oscars, including Best Picture and Best Director.

Oct 1995

"Coronation Street" stalwart and everyone's favourite barmaid Julie Goodyear left the show after 30 years.

Alamy.

Aug 1997

Reports emerged in the early hours of the morning that Diana, Princess Of Wales had been injured in a car crash in Paris which had claimed the life of Harrods heir Dodi Fayed. Within hours the tragic news came through that Diana had died of her injuries in hospital.

June 1999

The construction of the Millennium Dome was completed in Greenwich, south-east London.

iStock

On The Cover

The "Friend" weathered the storms of the Eighties – natural, marital and political – with ease . . .

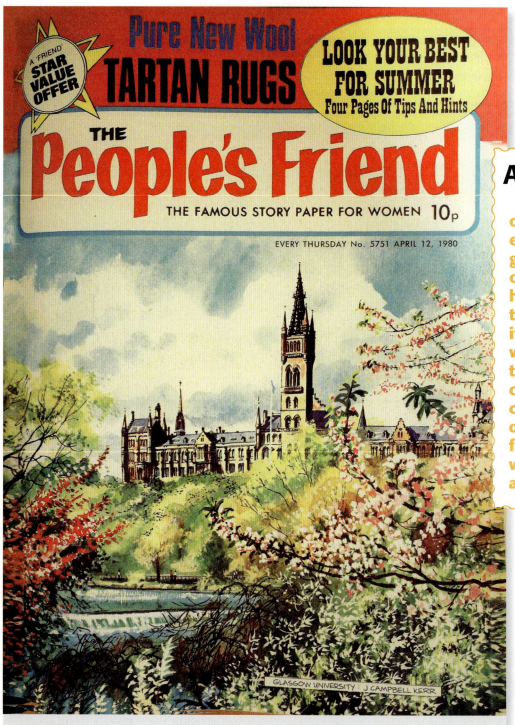

A 'FRIEND' STAR VALUE OFFER

Pure New Wool TARTAN RUGS

LOOK YOUR BEST FOR SUMMER Four Pages Of Tips And Hints

THE **People's Friend**

THE FAMOUS STORY PAPER FOR WOMEN 10p

EVERY THURSDAY No. 5751 APRIL 12, 1980

GLASGOW UNIVERSITY : J CAMPBELL KERR

April 12, 1980

The way people communicated was entering an era of great and powerful change. Who could have foretold, when the "Friend" began its journey, that it would live to see a time when readers could instantly send crystal-clear images of themselves, their families and their way of life from across the globe?

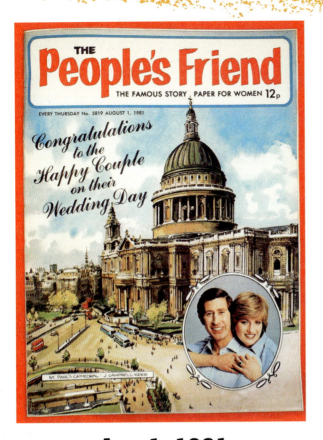

Aug 1, 1981

A bittersweet memory of a happy occasion.

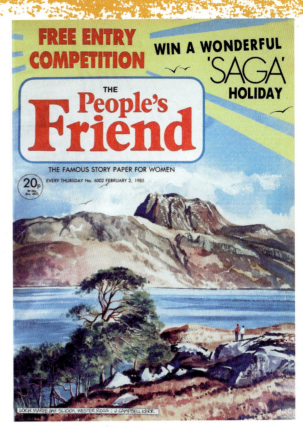

Feb 2, 1985

Competitions were as popular as they'd ever been.

Dec 23, 1989

Carrying on the royal theme with Glamis Castle.

June 6, 1992

Her Majesty celebrated 40 years on the throne.

John and Anne Taylor have been "fan favourites" since 1981.

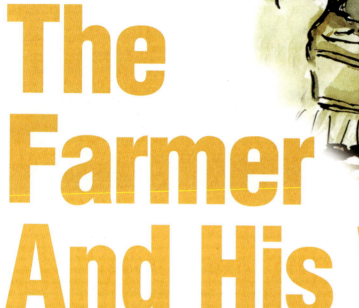

The Farmer And His Wife

When the "Friend" launched a new series, no-one imagined it would still be going strong 30 years on.

IN 1981, "The People's Friend" introduced a new "filler" feature to the magazine. It was called "The Farmer And His Wife" and was a series of couthy tales told by a fictional farmer named John Taylor.

To illustrate each story, one of the magazine's most

Doug Phillips at work.

popular freelance artists, a gentleman by the name of Doug Phillips, was called into service. In his unique, lively and observant style, Doug captured the warm and homely feel of the stories perfectly.

Douglas Phillips (1926-2012) was a Dundee lad born and bred, and proud of it. Although he had studied at Dundee Art College, he was working as an office boy in one of the jute mills when he was called up to the Army, to serve in India and Ceylon.

During this period he still managed to find time to paint and sketch, something which came to the attention of those higher up, and Doug soon found himself engaged in "tactical sketching" for the Army.

When he came back home to Dundee, Doug took a job in the Art

Department of D.C. Thomson & Co., but left to pursue a freelance career as an illustrator some years later.

Doug's great talent and his incredible work rate ensured he was never short of a commission. He illustrated over 100 children's books, produced covers for the "Reader's Digest" and exhibited lots of his own wonderful paintings.

But here at the "Friend" Doug is remembered with particular affection. He often dropped into the editorial office, and it was always good to see him.

The designers in particular relished his tales of the old days in the Meadowside Art Department, and the many colourful characters who worked there.

In addition to painting over 1,000 covers as

J. Campbell Kerr, Doug also found time to showcase his skills in the magazine's regular "From The Sketchbook Of . . ." feature, with captivating pen and ink drawings of some of the many places he loved to visit.

When the "Friend" underwent a redesign in 2015, new artwork was commissioned for the Farmer feature.

While this has proved popular, so many readers continued to express their affection for the original artwork that three volumes of the stories, illustrated by Doug, have now been published.

Doug did a lot of work for many of D.C. Thomson's publications, but there is no doubt that it was the "Friend" that won his heart.

He saw quite a few editors come and go, and he would be absolutely delighted to think that people were still enjoying his work and remembering him so fondly. ■

Dura Den
in Fife.

Willie Shand.

John Taylor's Fife

Regular readers will be familiar with the places John Taylor often visits on his jaunts around Fife. His farm is set within that lovely part of the Kingdom known as the East Neuk – a neuk being a niche or a corner.

Fife's climate and soils are well suited to arable farming, with large acreages under wheat, barley, oats, turnips, potatoes and all sorts of other vegetables and fruits.

You could drive through Fife and almost never see a cow or a sheep – John's few cross-breeds excepted, of course.

Up on the Riggin, they get a good blast of any wind as it blows in from the North Sea. Straight from Siberia, as John often tells us!

Far out across the Firth of Forth you'll see uninterrupted views to the Bass Rock and away to the Isle of May – a prospect John frequently enjoys from his own fields.

Bounded on three sides by the waters of the Firth of Tay, the North Sea and the Firth of Forth, Fife has no shortage of coastal attractions, rugged cliffs giving way to wide sheltered bays and inviting sandy beaches, punctuated every now and then by charming old fishing ports like Crail, Pittenweem, Anstruther and St Monans.

Whichever road you choose to follow, you don't go far before reaching another wee town or village with enough of interest to warrant stopping for a closer look.

Ceres is an old fermtoun steeped in stories from Fife's past. Above the Green stands a granite memorial to the men of Ceres who marched off to join the Bruce at Bannockburn in 1314.

Their return is still celebrated each year in Ceres at Scotland's oldest Highland Games.

St Andrews and Cupar are Fife's two principal towns and both have a long history. Cupar gained the status of County Town away back in 1214.

In the centre of Cupar, where the Crossgate and Bonnygate meet, stands the mercat cross, and close by is the old Corn Exchange, provided as a comfortable place for farmers to conduct the buying and selling of their agricultural products and implements.

Harvest can be a stressful time for those who rely on this as their main source of the year's income. Not many might welcome a return to the days of the Clydesdale horse, but keeping abreast of modern technology certainly doesn't come cheap.

Tractors have grown into different beasts since the old grey Fergie. Changed days indeed since John acquired his old Fordson with its cold and uncomfortable iron seat.

For all that, looking out from the summit of the Law, you might imagine the landscape of that area we've come to know as the Riggin is pretty much timeless.

The Early Days

"The Farmer And His Wife" made its debut in the issue dated May 2, 1981. The author of these stories was, in fact, an architect called Maurice Taylor.

He came from a farming background and drew on his knowledge and memories to create the world of the Riggin, set in the East Neuk of Fife.

Fife was a place Maurice knew a great deal about. In 1945 he became Chief Planning Officer there and spearheaded much of the development of modern Fife.

Maurice wrote as a hobby, and "The Farmer And His Wife" was intended as an occasional series which would appear for a couple of years.

But that was not how things turned out! Maurice's writing had a certain warmth and magic – he wrote as if he were chatting to friends round the kitchen table – and readers soon took John and Anne Taylor to their hearts.

John was a living person, hard-working, honest, a bit old-fashioned and rather too fond of his grub.

The readers sent Christmas cards, recipes and letters to this man with whom they felt such an affinity.

On the face of it, the stories of life on the Riggin were lighthearted articles which added a bit of fun. But the reality was that John Taylor's tales of days gone by inspired real affection and emotion in everyone who read them.

Over the years, various editors attempted to replace it with something new.

If it didn't appear, even for one week, letters would pour in, demanding to know what had happened to John Taylor.

Over 30 years later, these stories are still charming and entertaining readers all over the world.

Maurice himself sadly passed away in 1999 – but John and Anne Taylor live on.

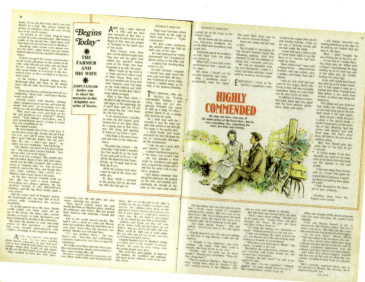

The 21st Century

The millennium marked a fresh optimism as the world celebrated. Looking to the future, the "Friend" embraced the digital world while holding strong to traditional values.

139

facebook

The People's
Friend Online

NEWS

CHAT TWEET

FOLLOW LIKE SHARE

Welcome To The Noughties

The millennium brought technological advances in all walks of life – and "Friend" readers had their own opinions on whether this was a good thing or not.

People's Friend

ANOTHER C...

Pe...ple's Friend

THE FAMOUS STORY MAGAZINE

EVERY THURSDAY No. 6811 AUGUST 5, 2000

54p
CANADA $3.2...

A Glorious Tribute
4-Page Pull-Out Inside

CAMPBELL KERR

THE "Noughties" marked a new century and a great many changes in the world.

The millennium issue of the "Friend" sported Edinburgh on the cover, known for its spectacular fireworks and New Year celebrations, and promised "marvellous Millennium reading", while the Editor summed up the thoughts of many when writing of a planned family party, finishing with the line: "Memories are every family's most precious heirlooms, to be treasured for ever . . ."

Inside, the new century was acknowledged with special recipes, and the doctor urged everyone to adopt a new outlook towards health, writing, "As you celebrate the brand-new millennium, resolve to start it with a whole new attitude to your health. List the health checks you've been avoiding and book an appointment now!"

This reflected a growing trend towards taking control of and responsibility for one's own health, which was probably influenced by the increasing amount of information accessible on the internet. An advertisement for the Imperial Cancer Fund was headed, "Turning cancer into hope" – an example of the huge advances being made in medicine.

With technology moving forward at great pace, "Friend" readers were reassured by the smiling face of Queen Elizabeth, the Queen Mother, whose portrait was on the cover as she celebrated her hundredth birthday.

The "Friend" also marked the occasion with a celebration pull-out, while advertisers offered commemorative gifts such as coins, videos, stamps and cross-stitch kits.

In 2002, the royal family lost Princess Margaret and, just a few weeks later, the Queen Mother. Alluding to the difficult time the royals had had over the past few years, the "Friend" referred to Her Majesty The Queen as "The Rock In The Storm".

A year later, the "Friend" invited readers to send in their messages to be included in a card which would be delivered to the Queen as she celebrated

2000-2010

Aug 2000
Queen Elizabeth The Queen Mother celebrated her 100th birthday.

Sept 2001
2,977 people perished when a series of attacks took place in America.

February 2002
The Queen celebrated her Golden Jubilee, marking 50 years since her ascension to the throne. The events were tinged with sadness in February when her sister, Princess Margaret, died following a stroke. There was more heartache the next month when the Queen's beloved mother passed away.

Jan 2003
The very last signal from NASA's Pioneer 10 spacecraft was received – some 7.6 billion miles from Earth!

her Golden Jubilee.

The "Friend" also offered a holiday to Windsor, a jubilee motif to embroider and a special cake to make and decorate. If that was too much activity, readers could sit back and relax with Judith Davis's specially written story, "Half A Century On . . ."

Meanwhile, the digital world was expanding. E-mail addresses and websites began to appear in features, and one competition told readers how useful it would be to

With technology moving forward at great pace, "Friend" readers were reassured by the smiling face of Queen Elizabeth, the Queen Mother

pay their phone bill with a new BT phone card.

Home computers and laptops quickly became more familiar in the home.

One proud granny wrote in to say she had studied computing at college, obtaining five SCOTVEC certificates along the way, and had taught her grandchildren how to surf the net. She had even invested in a PlayStation!

Mobile phones became more commonplace, too, though one reader did confess on the letters page that she rarely switched her phone on, while another wrote complaining of the growing trend of using a phone in the cinema.

In 2003 the Editor wrote about a friend changing her phone for a new smaller, lighter model that had a catchy ringtone and vibrated. We had no idea then that, 10 years on, people would be using phones to access the internet, take photographs and pay bills.

At times, it felt as if the new world was a much more dangerous place than the past. Horrific terrorism atrocities such as the Twin Towers on September 11, 2001 and the London bombings shook the world, and as a result we all became used to travel restrictions and longer security queues at airports.

But this did not deter people from travelling, and the "Friend" received many queries about the introduction of the Euro, and which European destinations were best.

On a lighter note, the "Friend" celebrated its 140th birthday in January 2009 with a specially written short story by Lisa Main, a compilation of highlights from the magazine, a cake and good wishes from readers and contributors.

In her column, the Editor promised, "We intend to reward you with many more years of great reading to come!"

Proof that some things never change! ■

The Rise Of Reality TV

The Noughties saw the rise of reality TV, beginning with "Castaway", which introduced the viewing public to Ben Fogle, whose career took off following his win.

Unlike many instant celebrities from programmes such as "Big Brother", Ben remained a working journalist and presenter and featured in the "Friend" over the years.

In general, "Friend" readers were not too impressed with celebrity status, though they would send in photographs of themselves when meeting someone well known.

One reader told us of her meeting with actress and "Friend" columnist Gwyneth Guthrie. She enclosed a photo in which Gwyneth had obliged by putting on her "Mrs Mack" from "High Road" face.

This decade saw TV chefs make guest appearances from time to time in the "Friend", including Loyd Grossman, Richard Cawley, Ross Burden, Lesley Waters, Antony Worrall Thompson and Keith Floyd. However, not all our readers approved. M.G. of Henlow wrote asking if there were any celebrity chefs able to cook plain and simple meals.

"I see dozens of cookery shows and not once has a good plate of simple stew or sausage, egg and chips been offered as a culinary delight," she wrote. Her letter continued with the suggestion that a cookery show featuring ordinary mums cooking would be a good idea.

Little did anyone know, that in the next decade, shows such as "The Great British Bake Off" and "Britain's Best Home Cook" would do just that.

Oct 2004

The Scottish Parliament building in Edinburgh, designed by Enric Miralles, was officially opened.

March 2005

BBC's "Doctor Who" returned to our screens after an absence of 16 years. Christopher Eccleston took control of the TARDIS.

July 2009

"Harry Potter And The Deathly Hallows" by J.K. Rowling, the final book in the Harry Potter franchise, was published. Since the first in the series was published in 1997, J.K. Rowling's novels have sold over 500 million copies worldwide, making them the best-selling book series in history.

April 2010

A cloud of volcanic ash from the eruption of Eyjafjallajökull in Iceland closed the airspace over the UK and northern and western Europe.

The People's Friend Online

NEWS
CHAT TWEET SHARE
FOLLOW LIKE

The Digital Age

The "Friend" has always kept pace with changing times – experience that stands it in good stead to this day.

AS the 21st century entered its teenage years, there was an explosion in the use of social media.

The "Friend", as ever, proved it could keep up with changing times by moving into the digital space on Facebook, Twitter and the internet.

The digital world gave readers the opportunity to connect with the magazine in new and immediate ways. Staff members featured in photographs and videos posted online,

and blogs revealed more of their personalities, likes and dislikes.

Celebrity bloggers might have ruled supreme in the wider world, but not in "Friend" land!

Official recognition of the magazine's achievements and contribution to the world of publishing came with a string of awards, including Magazine Of The Year in 2013.

This was a time of referendums – alternative voting, Scottish independence, European Union membership – but

the "Friend" remained neutral throughout, aware that readers would hold a variety of views.

Readers' opinions were, however, sought on various topics for a new Talking Point feature which covered recycling, queueing, Hallowe'en and a variety of other subjects, and encouraged lively debate.

Homecoming Year Scotland 2014 was a major event which the "Friend" supported with features and a special serial.

Inspired by the vast numbers of Scots who had emigrated to make new lives in countries such as the USA, Canada, South Africa, Australia and New Zealand, this was an opportunity for many families to visit and explore their roots and enjoy Scottish hospitality.

The royal family had good reasons to celebrate, with Prince William and Kate Middleton's marriage, and the births of Prince George, Princess Charlotte and Prince Louis.

The new Succession To

2011-2019

April 2011
An estimated two billion people across the globe watched the wedding of Prince William and Catherine Middleton.

March 2012
246 years after its first publication, the Encyclopaedia Brittanica stopped its print edition.

July 2013
Andy Murray won the Men's Singles title at Wimbledon. He defeated Novak Djokovic in straight sets. He became the first British man to win Wimbledon since Fred Perry in 1936. Murray went on to become Wimbledon champion again in 2016.

Aug 2014
British actor, director, producer and entrepreneur Sir Richard Attenborough died aged 90.

The Crown Act 2013 meant that male children no longer took precedence, so the young princess was fourth in succession between her older and younger brothers.

On May 19, 2018, the marriage of Prince Harry and Meghan Markle took place on a gloriously sunny day in Windsor. The public quickly took the new Duchess of Sussex to their hearts.

Understandably, the Queen decided to cut back

The "Friend" continued to listen to its readers, taking notice of what they wanted from a magazine

on public engagements, while Prince Philip retired from public life altogether at the age of ninety-six.

The "Friend" continued to mark the highlights of royal life, whilst at the same time showcasing the achievements of ordinary people doing extraordinary things.

Readers responded generously to charitable appeals, supporting smaller causes such as fishing boats for the Philippines and the Winnie

Working With Animals

Over the years the "Friend" has followed several assistance animals as they have undergone training.

The first pups were unsuccessful as Hearing Dogs and went on to be family pets instead. Ursa, however, became a Dog For The Disabled.

In 2011 "Friend" readers met Widget, a lively bundle of white fur, desperate to learn and to please.

Everyone was thrilled with his progress and delighted when he finally became a Canine Partners assistance dog.

Labrador sisters Nena and Nita, also training to be Canine Partners, gave readers much joy and they, too, made the grade as working dogs.

More recently the "Friend" followed the work of Riding For The Disabled. Toffee the pony showed promise but was found not to have the right temperament to be a success. He did, however, give readers much enjoyment as the "Friend" followed his progress.

And still with ponies, the "Friend" team were delighted to be paid a visit in 2017 by a pair of adorable miniature Shetland therapy ponies shortly after the magazine's move into D.C. Thomson's newly restored headquarters in Dundee city centre. They were our most unusual visitors to date!

Widget with his human partner, Esther.

Mabaso Foundation in South Africa alongside bigger charities like Age UK.

With interest rates at an all-time low and changes in pension legislation and benefits taking place, the "Friend" introduced a monthly finance page, reflecting its readers' desire to take control of their money and be aware of their options.

A move towards greener living and being more environmentally aware led to an increased focus on sustainable gardening, with experts John Stoa and Alexandra Campbell sharing their knowledge.

As has always been the case, the "Friend" continued to listen to its readers, taking notice of how their lives were changing and what they wanted from a magazine, and evolving the content and design to suit.

Opportunities for staff and readers to meet and talk face to face presented themselves at events and shows up and down the country, and in 2015 the "Friend" hosted its first writing workshop for aspiring authors. How the first Editor would have approved!

The first ever "Friend" holiday followed in 2018, with a bespoke weekend break in Cheshire enjoyed by staff and readers alike.

Such innovations could not have been dreamed of back in 1869 when the first issue was sent to press. But in spite of all the changes 150 years of progress have brought, the "Friend" remains to this day a true and constant friend to all its legions of readers worldwide. ■

May 2015
Charlotte Elizabeth Diana was born, a second child for the Duke and Duchess of Cambridge.

June 2016
The United Kingdom voted in a referendum to leave the European Union.

Feb 2018
Space X, the American aerospace manufacturer owned by billionaire Elon Musk, made a successful maiden flight from the John F. Kennedy Space Center. The rocket ship, called the Falcon Heavy, was launched into orbit with a Tesla Roadster car strapped to it! It was the first rocket of its kind that could return to Earth and be reused.

Jan 2019
Your beloved magazine reaches its 150th birthday! A true record-breaker!

On The Cover

The "Friend" has come a long way, but the journey's not over! Who knows where the next rise in the road will lead?

Competitions open to UK residents only, unless otherwise stated.

Polly Pullar's passion for the elusive pine marten

7 feel-good stories

Easy fish and seafood recipes

Aug 18, 2018 No. 7740

The People's Friend

£1.30

The best fiction!
- Anne Stenhouse's new serial set in a theatre
- A lively crime drama by Helen M. Walters

Indonesian Gado Gado Salad

Grilled Halibut with Strawberry-Mango Salsa

18-Aug-2018
£1.30
UK Off-sale date · 22-Aug-2018
AU $4.50, NZ $4.50
DC THOMSON MEDIA

Glorious
Glastonbury
Explore this lovely part of Somerset

Free Pattern Inside

Clever ways to transform a small garden

Money-off coupon for Maeve Haran's new book

Knit a snuggly blanket for Cats Protection

Aug 18, 2018

This lively front cover with its vibrant colours could not be more different from that of the first issue in 1869, and yet it's immensely reassuring to know that the trademark "Friend" blend of quality stories, practical advice and interesting articles on a whole range of diverse topics endures.

Feb 12, 2000

This tranquil spot seems unmoved by the new century.

Jan 15, 2005

A dramatic view of St Andrews, the home of golf.

March 23, 2013

A fresh look for a much-loved favourite.

Oct 31, 2015

An unusual cover design for this issue.

The "Friend" team would like to thank all the many friends, colleagues and contributors who helped make this Special Collector's Edition a reality. Putting it together required a great deal of painstaking research, and special thanks are due to the D.C. Thomson Archives team, who fielded our numerous requests for help and information with patience and good humour. We are also very grateful to Mr L.M. Thomson, Norman Watson, Peter Davidson and others for sharing their vast knowledge of D.C. Thomson's history.

Most of all, we want to thank all our readers past, present and future, without whom our beloved "Friend" would not be the success it is today. You are all a part of its amazing story.

Thank you!